simply shrimp, salmon, and (fish) steaks

Also by Leslie Glover Pendleton

One Dough, Fifty Cookies: Baking Favorite and Festive
Cookies in a Snap

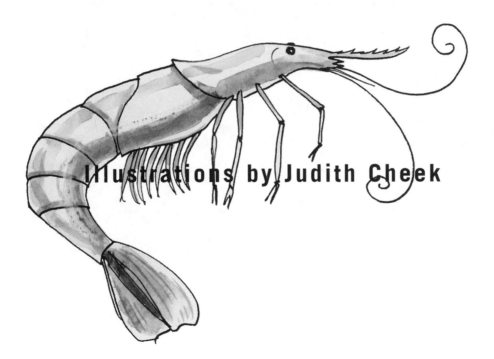

Illustrations by Judith Cheek

simply shrimp, salmon, and (fish) steaks

easy, delicious, and healthful ways to enjoy your favorite seafood plus side dishes to make a meal

Leslie Glover Pendleton

HarperCollins*Publishers*

HarperCollins books may be purchased for educational, business, or sales promotional use. For information please write: Special Markets Department, HarperCollins Publishers Inc., 10 East 53rd Street, New York, NY 10022.

FIRST EDITION

Designed by Elina D. Nudelman

Illustrations by Judith Cheek

Printed on acid-free paper

Library of Congress Cataloging-in-Publication Data

Pendleton, Leslie Glover.
    Simply shrimp, salmon, and (fish) steaks / Leslie Glover Pendleton — 1st ed.
        p. cm.
    ISBN 0–06–019337–9
    1. Cookery (Seafood) I. Title.

 TX747.P43   2000
 641.6'92 — dc21   99-055151

00 01 02 03 04 ❖/RRD 10 9 8 7 6 5 4 3 2 1

contents

thank-you notes   vii

introduction   ix

shrimp   xviii

salmon   56

fish steaks   112

simple sides   168

index   209

Thank-You Notes

Creating recipes, like dining, should never be done alone. The honest input I receive from family, friends, and colleagues is essential to make a cookbook useful to others. I am grateful to all who encourage and help me bring my recipes out of my mind and kitchen and onto paper.

Thank you to my testers and tasters: Dede, Tom, Connie, Pino, Mark, Kevin, Kath, Dennis, and all the guests around my table who were not allowed to get up until they made a critical comment. I am amazed and inspired by the diversity of my friends, and I thank them all for sharing their culinary heritage, especially Georgiana, Sallie, Laura, Miguel, Pino, and Sandra. As always, I thank my husband Mark, who is just starting to be able to enjoy seafood again, and my children, Will and Lydia, who never hesitate to offer their opinions.

Thank you to all the quality fish markets, especially Cameron Seafood Market in Silver Spring, Maryland; City Fish in Wethersfield, Connecticut, and the place where it all started, Rowayton Seafood in Rowayton, Connecticut. And finally, I thank my agent, Alice Martell, for getting it out there and my editor, Susan Friedland, for bringing it all together.

Introduction

Are you facing some nutritional facts of life and trying to find ways to incorporate healthy, tasty fish into your meat-and-potato-lover's diet? These quick and versatile recipes, using Americans' favorite catches of the day, are a great place to start. Seafood is an essential, healthy source of lean protein, containing oils that actually lower cholesterol, and saving time is essential to our fast-paced twenty-first-century lives. The recipes in this book offer you both of these benefits. The majority of them can be prepared in thirty minutes or less, and usually elements, if not the entire dish, can be made in advance.

Seafood, with its naturally tender flesh, absorbs seasonings well and cooks quickly, suiting it to myriad flavors and cooking techniques. Sauté quickly and your fish will be crisp and caramelized outside while silken and moist within, or slowly poach it in seasoned broth and it becomes delicate and aromatic. Whatever fish you choose for any occasion, complete your menu with the unique and even quicker side dishes in the last chapter.

By concentrating on shrimp, salmon, and (fish) steaks, the names stay the same no matter how you slice them or where you find them. The three S's are available everywhere in the United States in consistent quantity and quality, and supermarkets across the country almost always have one of them on special sale.

For twelve years I created roughly two hundred new recipes a year for *Gourmet* magazine. Now I create more than that annually for my own books and other clients, but there is a big difference. When I cook now, I do it in my kitchen, with no one to clean up after me, and with a limited time frame (before my children get home). My everyday conversations about food are no longer with professional cooks but home cooks, looking for fresh ideas to prepare simple meals. I am more than happy to oblige, since I too am always looking for delicious shortcuts.

As more fresh, high-quality ingredients become available, and even small-town restaurants feature worldwide cuisine, the American palate is more sophisticated than ever. With a recipe in hand and the vast assortment of ingredients available in our stores, we can prepare fresh, inexpensive, healthy, and tasty seafood dishes in our own kitchens.

Quick, healthy, and delicious food is within reach, so give it a try.

The most important thing to remember about buying seafood is to make sure it is fresh!

This does not mean you have to be on the docks when a catch comes in, but you do need to pay attention to what you are buying. Seafood in general should appear moist and firm, and have a clean seawater smell. There should be nothing "fishy"-smelling or -looking about your seafood purchase. Remember, most fish markets and other stores do not want to sell you an inferior product, because they want you to come back. If they don't seem interested in quality, find another store.

1. Do not hesitate to ask your store to cut you a fresh portion of fish from the cooler. You can also ask them when they get their seafood shipments. Plan your menus around the time you know there will be the freshest fish. Thursday is a common day for stores to receive fresh fish for the weekend.

2. Read the sell-by date on prepackaged fish and *do not* buy it if it is today's or tomorrow's date.

3. Thawed "previously frozen" fish or shrimp only means they've defrosted it for you, and you need to use it immediately. If you buy it frozen, you can defrost it yourself when you want to eat it.

4. Try to be flexible. If you had your heart set on halibut, but it looks tired next to the gleaming, firm tuna or sea bass, go with the freshest and try the halibut another time.

5. If you find that you have been sold an inferior product, please let your market know about it. This is the only way you can expect to receive quality fresh foods.

SHRIMP

There are so many varieties of shrimp sold in this country from all over the world that it is useless to try to judge a shrimp by its color or species. Even the sizes have gotten confusing. One supermarket's large shrimp might be classified "medium" by a fishmonger. In the business, shrimp are classified by the number of shrimp per pound, such as 35–40s (medium) or 21–25s (jumbo).

In most of the recipes I have called for a size range in the shrimp. For example: 2 pounds medium to extra large shrimp. There can be an enormous range in price, especially if one size is on sale, so I didn't want to confine a recipe to one size when another, at half the price, would be fine.

Unless you are near or on the docks where the shrimpers are bringing in their catch, you cannot buy "never been frozen" shrimp. Shrimp deteriorate very quickly and are usually frozen as soon as they are caught to preserve freshness. Cooking shrimp on the boat and eating them immediately would be the ultimate form of consumption, but most of us must settle for frozen. Again, this is something for which I've come to trust my supermarket, because they buy large quantities, sell large quantities, and can offer good prices. Shopping clubs or warehouses often have the best prices. I buy frozen bags of shrimp to thaw myself, as needed. Otherwise, look for intact, firm-fleshed shrimp that have been recently thawed (ask). A strong "fishy" or ammonia odor is a sign of deterioration. Once thawed, use the shrimp within twenty-four hours.

When following a recipe, any size shrimp can usually be substituted, but take into account that the cooking time will change. The larger the shrimp, the higher the price, unless there is a special sale. Often the price dictates my purchase, unless I'm doing a special dish such as Grilled Butterflied Jumbo Shrimp, which requires shrimp the size of small lobster tails.

Deveining shrimp is a matter of preference. Sometimes I remove and sometimes I don't. Small shrimp have small veins, hardly worth the time it takes to remove them, while larger shrimp can have large, sometimes gritty veins. To determine what to do, make a shallow slit down the backs of a few shrimp, remove the veins, and see if they are large, dark, and gritty. If they are, then devein the remaining shrimp. If they are white, pink, or almost nonexistent, I wouldn't bother deveining them all.

SALMON

Thanks to the vast quantities of pale-orange-fleshed, farm-raised Atlantic salmon, the whole country can enjoy fresh steaks and fillets year-round at great prices. I have found that the fresh (never-been-frozen) salmon available in the seafood section of my supermarket is of consistent quality and supply. There is no reason to buy "previously frozen" salmon, for any price. It's not worth it. Only recently have I begun to trust the seafood sections of supermarkets, but as the demand for fish has risen, so has the demand for good quality.

Don't be pressured into buying prepackaged portions of fish when you can have your order cut in front of you and skinned, if necessary for the recipe. If you must buy by the package, check the sell-by date. Markets usually give themselves four to five days to sell, so make sure you are buying at least two days before the date on the package.

Salmon connoisseurs will argue over which salmon is supreme, especially on the Pacific coast, where different varieties of line-caught salmon are available in different seasons. If you are lucky enough to have choices in the fresh line-caught category, then please compare. Otherwise, buy what looks good and fresh.

FISH STEAKS

Any large fish can be cut crosswise through the spine into steaks. In different regions with different ethnic populations you can find different fish steaks. In this book you will find recipes using halibut, swordfish, tuna, and salmon steaks, but any fresh steak fish can be substituted.

Halibut is a large flat fish with a delicate, firm, white flesh. It is usually sold in steaks but can also be found in one-and-a-half-to-two-inch-thick fillets. The elongated steaks are divided into four sections by large bones that can easily be removed after cooking. Fillets can be substituted in the recipes, except when grilling, when fillets fall apart too easily.

Swordfish is not worth cooking if the only option is previously frozen steaks, as this turns the firm, meaty flesh into mush. Unlike shrimp and salmon, I rarely find good fresh swordfish in the supermarket. Your local fish market is the best place to look for swordfish, unless your supermarket has a specific special on *fresh*, never-been-frozen swordfish steaks.

When purchasing, check that the steaks are firm, with a symmetrical red streak of flesh in the middle. (It resembles a flying bird or an M shape.) The skin should be smooth, with little fat underneath. If the skin is thick and rough like sandpaper and the red flesh is in large round sections, you are probably being sold shark. Shark steaks are a perfect substitute for swordfish, but they should be about half the price.

Tuna is a favorite of those who don't love fish as well as those who do. Its dark flesh and meaty taste and texture are suited for bolder marinades and sauces. Tuna steaks, if very fresh, firm, and not overcooked, are the ultimate fish indulgence. The flesh is so lean it must be served pink in the middle, or you might as well open a can. I cook my tuna rare in the middle, but my husband prefers it medium—that is, cooked until there is only a thin red line through the middle (usually visible on the side of the steak). If you cannot or will not eat pink tuna, then substitute swordfish or shark, which must never be cooked rare.

A NOTE ON OVERFISHING

Advances in technology allow fishing fleets to go farther, longer, and deeper, making commercial fishing more efficient. At the same time this puts a strain on the stocks of fish in the oceans, especially the Atlantic. The International Convention for the Conservation of Atlantic Tunas (ICCAT) sets the quotas allowable for fishing large migratory species in the entire Atlantic, according to the "sustainability" of the fish stocks. The United States is a member of this convention and abides by its restrictions. The U.S. also has considerable influence in the implementation of future laws and restrictions adopted by ICCAT, as do the other member nations.

In 1998 the Natural Resources Defense Council (NRDC) and Sea Web, a marine education initiative funded by the multimillion-dollar Pew Charitable Trusts, chose to focus attention on the popular swordfish, out of the one hundred threatened species in the Atlantic. The "give swordfish a break" campaign called on restaurants and the public to stop serving and eating the fish for one year. The goal of the campaign (never meant as a boycott, but a temporary time-out), was to promote effective government action to restore North Atlantic swordfish stocks, and to raise awareness of our fragile ocean resources. While the action did advertise the problem, it also hurt the American swordfishing fleet, which was already in compliance with current restrictions.

Pacific swordfish and yellowfin tuna are being harvested at sustainable levels. The endangered bluefin tuna, in demand for sushi, is not available to the average consumer.

This is an ongoing, complex, worldwide issue, so what is the consumer to do? Buying U.S.-certified fish from a reputable dealer is the best way to support a legitimate fishing industry obeying harvesting restrictions. Uncertified fish is not inspected and could have been caught by anyone, anywhere.

KEYS TO SUCCESS

There are four basic ways to cook your fresh seafood and a couple of hints to make each successful. The most important rule overall is: Do not overcook. Seafood is an invaluable source of healthy lean protein, and when foods high in lean protein—including beef, chicken breast, and white-meat pork—are overcooked, they dry out. The difference between the best fish you have ever tasted and the worst can come down to a couple of minutes too long on the heat. Once you get used to a properly cooked fish, you will no longer accept a dried-out expensive entrée at a restaurant.

Determining whether fish is done by touching it takes practice. Do not hesitate to cut into the center of the flesh to see if it is opaque. As soon as it stops looking raw in the middle, remove it from the heat, as it will still cook slightly afterward.

1. Sautéed or fried

Key to success: Use a nonstick pan and, if deep-frying, make sure the oil is the correct temperature.

2. Grilled or broiled

Key to success: Oil the preheated grill and the fish. If broiling, preheat the broiler and use the rack closest to the heat.

3. Steamed/Boiled/Poached/Stewed

Key to success: Cook gently.

4. Roasted or baked

Key to success: Use high heat for roasting, and for both, do not overcook.

shrimp

Simply Boiled Shrimp

A New Shrimp Cocktail

Shrimp, Jicama, and Avocado Salad with Cumin Grapefruit Dressing

Cilantro Shrimp with Peanut Dip

Buffalo Shrimp

Grilled Margarita Shrimp Fajitas

Pickled Shrimp with Wasabi

Sautéed Shrimp with Black Bean Sauce

Grilled Shrimp Wrapped in Hot Cappicola and Basil

Grilled Tandoori-Style Shrimp with Mint Chutney

Orange-Glazed Shrimp with Gingered Cucumber Salsa

Caesar Shrimp, Tomato, and Artichoke Heart Kebabs

Grilled Butterflied Shrimp with Pineapple Scallion-Butter Sauce

Big-Easy Shrimp

Stir-Fried Shrimp and Broccoli

Baked Shrimp Pesto

Tsatsiki Shrimp Salad

Roasted Shrimp, Potatoes, and Prosciutto Portuguese-Style

Shrimp Stuffed with Pita, Spinach, Sun-Dried Tomatoes, and Almonds

Shrimp and Sausage Jambalaya

Shrimp in Greek Tomato Herb and Feta Sauce

Shrimp and Artichoke Fettuccine Alfredo

Shrimp with Broccoli Rabe, Bacon, and Pasta

Simply Spiced Shrimp

Curried Shrimp with Sweet Onions

Cornmeal Fried Shrimp

Deviled Shrimp

Crisp Sesame Shrimp

Crisp Coconut Graham Shrimp

Shrimp Pot Pie

simply boiled shrimp

There is additional sweet shrimp flavor contained in shrimp shells, therefore you get better flavor when shrimp are cooked with their shells on. However, if time is of the essence, the convenience of buying prepeeled shrimp may be worth the slight loss in flavor.

any size raw shrimp, thawed or frozen, with the shells on

In a large kettle, bring 3 inches of cold water to a boil. Add the shrimp, cover the pot, and cook over high heat, stirring occasionally, 1 minute for small shrimp up to 6 minutes for jumbos. The shrimp are done when all have curled and turned pink. Rinse shrimp under cold water to stop the cooking, and peel.

NOTE: Shrimp keep better cooked than raw. They should be cooked as soon as possible after thawing (1 day maximum). Once cooked, they can be kept covered and refrigerated for 2 days.

It is not recommended to reheat cooked shrimp, unless they can be heated quickly by adding to a hot sauce. Chilled boiled shrimp are best served in shrimp cocktail or salad.

a new shrimp cocktail

The classic tomato and horseradish sauce for shrimp is still a favorite, but this roasted-pepper version is a nice change. A snap to prepare using frozen precooked and peeled shrimp, this makes an impressive hors d'oeuvre. It also makes a great dressing for seafood salad.

1 7-ounce jar roasted red bell peppers, drained
2 teaspoons drained bottled horseradish
2 tablespoons mayonnaise
1 teaspoon Worcestershire sauce
1 teaspoon Old Bay Seasoning, or other "shrimp and crab boil" spice mix
1 teaspoon fresh lemon juice
salt
freshly ground black pepper

In a blender combine all the ingredients except salt and pepper and puree until smooth. Season with salt and pepper. Serve with Simply Boiled Shrimp (see page 2). The sauce keeps covered in the refrigerator for up to 5 days.

Makes ¾ cup

shrimp, jicama, and avocado salad with cumin grapefruit dressing

This is a refreshing one-dish meal for a hot summer night.

THE DRESSING

⅓ cup fresh grapefruit juice

1 tablespoon white wine vinegar

1 teaspoon honey

½ teaspoon ground cumin

¼ cup vegetable oil

salt

freshly ground black pepper

1 ripe avocado

2 cups watercress sprigs, washed and spun dry

1 small jicama, peeled and cut into ¼-inch-thick sticks (about 2 cups)

2 pounds Simply Boiled Shrimp (see page 2)

In a bowl, whisk together the dressing ingredients until emulsified. The dressing keeps covered in the refrigerator for 2 days.

Halve, pit, and peel the avocado. Cut it into 1-inch chunks. Divide the watercress among four plates and top it with the jicama and avocado.

Arrange the shrimp on top of the vegetables and drizzle with dressing. Serve immediately.

NOTE: If you are short of time, buy shrimp already peeled and cooked.

You can cook the shrimp and make the dressing 1 day in advance and keep them covered in the refrigerator.

Jicama (pronounced *HEE-ka-mah*) is crunchy, juicy, and slightly sweet, tasting like a cross between a raw potato and an apple. Diced, sliced, shredded, or cooked, jicama keeps its crunch and doesn't discolor once cut. Available year-round, it can vary from the size of an apple to that of a melon. Its beige skin should be as unblemished as possible, without soft spots.

Serves 4

cilantro shrimp with peanut dip

These tasty Southeast Asian–inspired shrimp make an unusual hors d'oeuvre. Serve the sauce in individual dipping pots when serving as a main course. Basmati or jasmine rice with Gingered Spaghetti Squash (page 196) make it a meal.

2 pounds raw medium to large shrimp, peeled

2 cups lightly packed fresh cilantro sprigs

2 tablespoons fresh lime juice

2 tablespoons olive oil

½ teaspoon salt

THE SAUCE

¼ cup chunky-style peanut butter

1 teaspoon sugar

½ teaspoon curry powder

2 tablespoons fresh lime juice

2 tablespoons light soy sauce

1 to 2 tablespoons water

⅛ teaspoon cayenne pepper

Put the shrimp in a bowl.

In a blender puree the cilantro, lime juice, oil, and salt and stir it into the shrimp. Cover and refrigerate for at least 30 minutes, up to 8 hours.

In a small bowl whisk together the ingredients for the sauce, adding enough water to reach the consistency of a thin mayonnaise.

Preheat the broiler, with the oven rack set on the top level.

Spread the shrimp in a single layer in a large jelly-roll pan and broil the shrimp for about 5 minutes, turning them once, until they are cooked through.

Serve the shrimp with the peanut sauce.

NOTE: Alternatively the shrimp can be threaded onto skewers and grilled on a preheated oiled grill for the same amount of time.

Serves 8 as a first course or 4 as a main dish

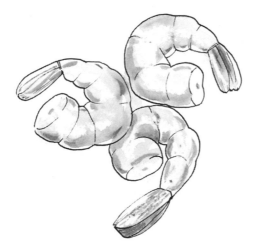

buffalo shrimp

These fried shrimp smothered in a rich spicy sauce were inspired by the now-classic American favorite, Buffalo chicken wings. Perhaps this isn't the healthiest dish, but without the chicken fat it is healthier than wings. Shrimp also provides a dignified alternative, while still satisfying a craving for something hot, messy, and bad.

2 tablespoons butter

1 tablespoon hot red pepper sauce (see Note)

1 tablespoon vinegar, or to taste

vegetable oil for frying

1½ pounds raw medium to large shrimp, peeled

¼ cup all-purpose flour

ACCOMPANIMENTS

celery sticks

Buffalo Shrimp Dip (recipe follows) or a premium bottled blue cheese or ranch dressing

In a large saucepan melt the butter. Off the heat, add the hot sauce and vinegar to taste and reserve.

In a deep fryer or kettle, heat 1 inch of vegetable oil to 375°F. Toss the shrimp with the flour until coated thoroughly. Fry the shrimp in small batches in the oil for 1 minute or until cooked through, and let the oil return to 375°F before adding the next batch. Drain the shrimp on paper towels and add them to the sauce, tossing to coat well.

Serve the shrimp immediately with the celery and dip.

NOTE: Some of the sauces made especially for hot chicken wings already have the extra vinegar added, and have varied levels of "heat." For example, once I used 5 tablespoons of Frank's Red Hot Sauce and omitted the vinegar, but another time I used 1 tablespoon Tabasco with 1 tablespoon vinegar. The latter was hotter. There are so many hot sauces on the market, especially "hot wings" sauces, that you must rely on your taste buds to determine how much to use.

Frying small batches of the shrimp at a time allows the oil to stay hot, keeps the shrimp crispy, and lets the oil return to 375°F quickly.

Serves 8 as a first course or 4 as a main dish

buffalo shrimp dip

This feta dressing is also delicious on salads or as a dip for vegetables.

½ cup sour cream (reduced-fat can be used)
½ cup mayonnaise (reduced-fat can be used)
½ cup crumbled feta cheese
1 teaspoon Worcestershire sauce
2 teaspoons white wine vinegar or lemon juice
¼ cup minced fresh chives or parsley leaves
salt
freshly ground black pepper

In a bowl, whisk all the ingredients together and season with salt and pepper. Covered and refrigerated, the dressing will keep for up to 3 days.

Makes about 1 ¼ cups

grilled margarita shrimp fajitas

You provide the grilled shrimp, warm tortillas, and colorful bowls of accompaniments. Your guests make their own fajitas by wrapping their tortillas around the irresistible selection of tastes and textures. Including your guests in the cooking process produces a jovial, relaxed atmosphere where the food becomes entertainment. Quick Rice and Beans (page 178) is an obvious accompaniment.

2 tablespoons tequila

1 tablespoon triple sec or orange juice

2 tablespoons lime juice

3 tablespoons vegetable oil

½ teaspoon freshly ground black pepper

1½ pounds raw medium to large shrimp, peeled

1 teaspoon coarse kosher or sea salt

8 6-to-8-inch flour tortillas

ACCOMPANIMENTS

2 small ripe avocados, sliced just before serving

chopped tomatoes

chopped red onion or scallion

sour cream

salsa

chopped fresh cilantro

lime wedges

Whisk together the tequila, triple sec, lime juice, oil, and pepper in a medium bowl. Add the shrimp, tossing to coat completely with the marinade. Chill the shrimp, covered, for 15 minutes to 1 hour.

Preheat a grill, or broiler with rack in the top position.

Remove shrimp from marinade, threading them onto metal skewers. Discard the marinade.

Sprinkle the shrimp with the salt. Brush the grill with vegetable oil and grill the shrimp skewers (or broil them on a rack set in a baking pan) for about 5 minutes on each side, or until just cooked through.

While the shrimp are cooking, grill (or broil right on the oven rack) the tortillas for about 1 minute on each side, transferring them to a brown paper bag to keep warm.

Remove the shrimp from the skewers and serve them with the warm tortillas for diners to wrap them, with the accompaniments, as desired.

NOTE: The liquor in the marinade may be omitted with equally delicious results.

Serves 4 as a main course or 6 to 8 as an appetizer

pickled shrimp with wasabi

Years ago I sampled my first southern-style pickled shrimp, prepared by a friend from Savannah, and it remains one of my favorite
hors d'oeuvres. As a variation, I add a Japanese twist to the dish with
wasabi powder, soy sauce, and cucumber. The fact that there is no
added fat is just a fringe benefit to the sparkling flavors.

¼ cup white wine vinegar

½ cup water

1 tablespoon soy sauce

1 teaspoon sugar

¼ teaspoon salt

1½ pounds raw small to medium shrimp, peeled

2½ teaspoons wasabi powder (see Note)

1 small red bell pepper, sliced thin

1 small onion, sliced thin

¼ cup lime or lemon juice

1 small cucumber, peeled, seeded, and sliced ¼ inch thick

toast or Saltine crackers as accompaniment

In a large saucepan combine the vinegar, water, soy sauce, sugar,
and salt. Bring mixture to a boil, add shrimp, and cook over high heat
until the shrimp just curl, about 2 minutes.

Remove from the heat and stir in the wasabi powder, bell pepper, and onion. Add the lime juice and cucumber and transfer the mixture to a glass or ceramic bowl just large enough to hold it. Cover, refrigerate, and let the shrimp marinate 4 to 24 hours. Serve with the crackers.

NOTE: Wasabi is powdered pale green Japanese horseradish. When mixed with water it forms the pungent spicy paste that accompanies Japanese sushi. One small jar goes a long way! Many supermarkets carry this in their ethnic or gourmet foods section.

Serves 6 to 8 as an appetizer

sautéed shrimp with black bean sauce

This dish is not only great tasting, it is a feast for the eyes. The combination of the bed of black bean sauce topped with pink shrimp, and highlighted with bright green cilantro, makes an irresistible appetizer. For a fine main course serve with rice, Braised Escarole with Tomatoes and Garlic (page 184), or Cucumber and Onion Salad with Yogurt Cumin Vinaigrette (page 202).

1 15-ounce can black beans
1 large garlic clove, minced
5 tablespoons olive oil
1 teaspoon chili powder
1½ cups canned chicken broth
1½ to 2 pounds raw medium to jumbo shrimp, peeled
salt
freshly ground black pepper
minced fresh cilantro (optional)

Drain the beans in a colander. Rinse them well.

In a skillet, cook the garlic in 2 tablespoons of olive oil over moderately low heat until the garlic begins to color. Add the chili powder and cook, stirring, for 30 seconds. Add the beans and cook, stirring, for 3 minutes. Stir in the broth, then transfer one cup of the mixture to a blender. Puree the mixture and return it to the skillet. Simmer the sauce, stirring, for 5 minutes and reserve.

Heat the remaining 3 tablespoons of oil in a large skillet over moderately high heat. Pat the shrimp dry and season with salt and pepper. Sauté the shrimp, in batches, for 2 minutes or until they are a pale golden color.

Heat the sauce and pour it in a shallow serving dish. Arrange the shrimp on top and sprinkle with the cilantro if desired.

NOTE: The sauce can be made 1 day in advance and kept, covered, in the refrigerator.

Alternatively the shrimp can be threaded onto skewers and grilled on a preheated oiled grill for the same amount of time. Pull the shrimp off the skewers and lay them on the sauce to serve.

Serves 4 as a main course or 6 as an appetizer

grilled shrimp wrapped in hot cappicola and basil

No matter how many shrimp I buy, there are never too many of these. I have seen perfectly polite people get downright aggressive in pursuit of their share of these shrimp right off the barby. They make a special appetizer, or serve as a main dish with Grilled Ratatouille Salad (page 186) and rice pilaf.

about 20 bamboo skewers
1½ pounds raw large shrimp
¼ pound very thin slices hot cappicola
30 to 40 fresh basil leaves
¼ cup fresh lime or lemon juice
2 tablespoons olive oil
salt
freshly ground black pepper

Soak the bamboo skewers in water for 1 hour to prevent them from burning on the grill.

Wrap each shrimp in a basil leaf and a half slice of cappicola, weaving them onto the skewers. Arrange the skewers on a tray.

In a small bowl, whisk together the lime juice and oil, and brush the skewers with the mixture. Sprinkle the shrimp with salt and pepper, and let them marinate for 15 minutes, no longer.

Preheat a grill, or broiler with rack in the top position.

Brush the grill with oil and grill the skewers (or broil them on a rack set in a baking pan) for 5 minutes on each side or until the shrimp are cooked through.

NOTE: To prepare ahead, thread the shrimp, basil, and cappicola up to 6 hours ahead and keep chilled, but do not marinate until 15 minutes before grilling.

Serves 6 as an appetizer or 4 as a main course

grilled tandoori-style shrimp with mint chutney

Sometimes very large shrimp are available (4 to 6 per pound). This is an impressive way to prepare those small-lobster-tail-sized delicacies, which serve about two per person. These shrimp are marinated with a "dry rub," spices that cling to the shrimp and are sealed in with the oil. For a main course, serve with basmati rice or Couscous with Dried Cranberries and Buttered Almonds (page 175) and/or Cucumber and Onion Salad with Yogurt Cumin Vinaigrette (page 202).

1½ pounds raw jumbo or extra-large shrimp, peeled
1 teaspoon turmeric
1 teaspoon sweet paprika
½ teaspoon coarse salt
¼ teaspoon pepper
1 tablespoon vegetable oil
Mint Chutney as an accompaniment (recipe follows)

Butterfly the shrimp by halving them lengthwise, through the rounded side, without cutting all the way through, but enough so that you can open them.

In a large bowl, combine the turmeric, paprika, salt, and pepper. Add the shrimp, tossing to coat them with spices. Add the oil and toss to coat well.

Preheat a grill, or broiler with rack in the top position.

Brush the grill with oil and grill the shrimp opened flat (or broil them on a rack set in a baking pan) for 5 minutes per side or until cooked through. Serve with the chutney.

NOTE: Smaller shrimp can be used. Thread the butterflied shrimp onto two parallel skewers to make it easier to turn them and to keep the shrimp open.

Serves 4

mint chutney

½ cup chopped onion
1 tablespoon olive oil
¼ cup chopped golden raisins
3 tablespoons wine vinegar
¼ cup water
¼ teaspoon dried hot red pepper flakes
¼ teaspoon ground coriander seed
¼ teaspoon salt
½ cup packed mint leaves

In a small skillet, cook the onion in oil over moderate heat, stirring, until pale golden. Add the raisins, vinegar, water, pepper flakes, coriander, and salt; simmer for 2 minutes. Transfer the mixture to a bowl and stir in the mint.

NOTE: The chutney keeps at room temperature for 8 hours, or covered in the refrigerator for 1 week.

Makes about 1¼ cups

orange-glazed shrimp with gingered cucumber salsa

This Asian-inspired dish is a dazzling mix of clean, crisp flavors. The sweet orange and hot pepper flakes on the shrimp are complemented by the sour lime and cool cucumber in the salsa. Add Charred Soy and Sesame String Beans (page 183) and rice and the menu is complete.

1 teaspoon freshly grated orange zest

⅓ cup fresh orange juice

2 tablespoons soy sauce

⅛ to ¼ teaspoon dried hot red pepper flakes

1 teaspoon cornstarch

1 pound raw large shrimp, peeled and deveined

Gingered Cucumber Salsa (recipe follows)

In a small saucepan, whisk together the orange zest and juice, soy sauce, pepper flakes, and cornstarch until blended. Add the shrimp and stir to coat with the marinade. Let marinate, covered and refrigerated, for 15 minutes to 1 hour.

Remove the shrimp from the marinade. Thread them onto metal skewers. Bring the marinade to a boil and simmer, stirring, for 2 minutes (see note).

Preheat a grill, or broiler with rack in the top position.

Brush the grill with vegetable oil and grill the skewers (or broil them on a rack set in a baking pan), for about 5 minutes on each side, basting with boiled marinade occasionally. Serve the shrimp with Gingered Cucumber Salsa.

NOTE: To avoid the step of threading the shrimp, jumbo shrimp or larger can be substituted. They are large enough to grill individually without falling through the grill.

Basting while cooking is a great way to add more flavor to food. However, it is very important to boil the marinade for at least 2 minutes before basting, to kill any bacteria present after marinating the raw fish.

Serves 2 as a main course or 4 as an appetizer

gingered cucumber salsa

2 cucumbers, peeled, seeded, and diced (about 2 cups)
1 tablespoon minced peeled ginger root
1 garlic clove, minced
⅔ cup chopped onion
¼ cup lime juice
3 tablespoons finely chopped fresh cilantro
¼ teaspoon salt
freshly ground black pepper

In a bowl, stir together the salsa ingredients. Keep the salsa covered and chill for 15 minutes.

NOTE: The salsa can be made 1 day in advance; keep it covered in the refrigerator.

Makes about 2½ cups

caesar shrimp, tomato, and artichoke heart kebabs

The United States has an ongoing love affair with Caesar salad. It has been elevated to main-course status in many restaurants, which offer it topped with chicken, steak, shrimp, or even fried calamari. The key to the Caesar's popularity is in the robust dressing, which is used—minus the raw egg—here to flavor shrimp and vegetables on the grill.

CAESAR MARINADE

    4 garlic cloves
    ½ cup olive oil
    ¼ cup fresh lemon juice
    1 tablespoon Worcestershire sauce
    1 teaspoon salt
    ½ teaspoon freshly ground black pepper
    ½ teaspoon dried oregano
    1 flat anchovy fillet (optional)

    1½ pounds raw large shrimp, peeled
    1 14-ounce can whole artichoke hearts (7 or 8 small hearts), halved
    16 cherry tomatoes

In a blender or food processor, combine all the marinade ingredients and blend until emulsified.

Thread the shrimp onto metal skewers, alternating them with the artichoke halves and tomatoes. Allow about 2 tomatoes and 2 artichoke halves per skewer.

Arrange the kebabs on a tray and drizzle them with half the marinade. The kebabs can be grilled immediately or covered and refrigerated for up to 2 hours.

Preheat a grill, or broiler with rack in the top position.

Brush the grill with vegetable oil, and grill the kebabs (or broil them on a rack set in a baking pan) for about 5 minutes on each side, brushing occasionally with the remaining marinade.

NOTE: Larger shrimp cost more, but there are fewer to thread on skewers, so the choice is yours. More time or more money?

Serves 4

grilled butterflied shrimp with pineapple scallion-butter sauce

This recipe is as versatile as the perfect basic black dress. You can dress it up for entertaining or dress it down and watch the kids gobble it up. A green salad and Basmati Rice, Currant, and Carrot Salad, (page 180) or Toasted Vermicelli and Herbs (page 176) round out the meal.

1½ pounds raw shrimp (large to jumbo), peeled

2 tablespoons vegetable oil

coarse kosher or sea salt

freshly ground black pepper

½ cup minced scallions

2 teaspoons white wine vinegar or lemon juice

¾ cup (6 ounces) pineapple juice

3 tablespoons butter

1 pinch cayenne pepper

Butterfly the shrimp by halving them lengthwise through the rounded side without cutting all the way through. You must be able to open them.

Thread about 4 shrimp onto two parallel thin metal skewers or pre-soaked bamboo skewers, opening the shrimp flat and threading them crosswise so they are lined up side by side (see note). Thread the remaining shrimp onto skewers in the same manner. Arrange the skewers on a platter. Coat the shrimp with the oil. Season with salt and pepper; keep covered and refrigerated until ready to grill, up to 4 hours.

In a medium saucepan, boil the pineapple juice until it is reduced to $\frac{1}{2}$ cup. Add the scallions and vinegar and simmer 1 minute more. Remove the pan from the heat and stir in the butter, cayenne, and salt, stirring until the butter is melted and sauce is thickened.

Preheat a grill, or broiler with rack in the top position.

Brush the grill with vegetable oil and grill shrimp skewers (or broil them on a rack set in a baking pan) 3 to 5 minutes on each side, or until just cooked through.

Serve the shrimp on the skewers, napped with the sauce, or remove them from the skewers and toss them with the sauce, or serve the sauce in individual dipping pots.

NOTE: Using two parallel skewers keeps the shrimp from closing or spinning when you turn them on the grill. If you use bamboo skewers, immerse them in water for at least 30 minutes to prevent them from burning during cooking.

Serves 4

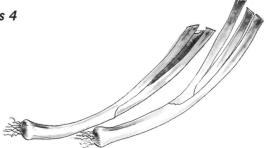

big-easy shrimp

The first time I ordered barbecued shrimp, in New Orleans, I was expecting something grilled, or sweet and saucy, or both. What I got was a delightful, spicy, and decadent surprise (what I should have expected in the first place). Crusty bread and a salad are all that's needed in addition to create an extraordinary meal. Put on some Buckwheat zydeco or Cajun jazz and sop up those buttery, garlicky, peppery-hot juices with abandon.

1½ pounds raw large shrimp (about 48), peeled and deveined
4 tablespoons butter
2 teaspoons chili powder
1½ teaspoons freshly ground black pepper
½ teaspoon dried oregano
2 large garlic cloves, minced
1 tablespoon Worcestershire sauce
⅓ cup dry white or red wine
¾ teaspoon salt
Crusty bread

Preheat the oven to 450°F.

Arrange the shrimp in a shallow baking dish just large enough to hold them in one layer or divide them evenly among four individual baking dishes.

Combine the remaining ingredients (except bread) in a saucepan and simmer for 5 minutes. Pour this sauce over the shrimp, stirring to coat them well, and bake for 10 to 12 minutes or until shrimp are just firm. Serve the shrimp with crusty bread.

NOTE: This dish can be assembled ahead of time. Make the sauce and let it cool. Combine the shrimp and sauce in a dish as directed, and keep covered and refrigerated until ready to bake, up to 8 hours.

Serves 4 as a main course or 8 as a first course

stir-fried shrimp and broccoli

Stir-fries are a convenient, orderly way to cook, in that all of the ingredients must be assembled ahead of time so that each can be added without delay during the quick, high-heat cooking process. The actual cooking is done just before serving, to ensure that the food will be hot and fresh tasting.

1 pound broccoli

1 cup canned chicken broth

2 tablespoons soy sauce

1 tablespoon rice vinegar

1 tablespoon sugar

1 tablespoon cornstarch

2 teaspoons minced peeled fresh ginger root

1 small onion

2 tablespoons vegetable oil

1½ pounds raw small to large shrimp, peeled

salt

freshly ground black pepper

3 cups cooked rice (1 cup uncooked)

Cut the broccoli florets into bite-size pieces, peel the stems, and cut them into thick slices. Blanch the broccoli in boiling water for 1 to 2 minutes or until barely tender. Drain and rinse under cold water.

In a measuring cup, stir together the broth, soy sauce, vinegar, sugar, cornstarch, and ginger.

Halve the onion lengthwise and slice it thinly lengthwise.

In a wok or large heavy skillet, heat the oil over high heat until very hot. Add the shrimp and onion and stir-fry for 1 minute or until the shrimp just turn pink. Stir the sauce mixture and add it to the skillet. Simmer 2 minutes, stirring; add the broccoli. Cook until the broccoli is heated through. Season with salt and pepper, and serve over the rice.

Serves 4

baked shrimp pesto

Here is one way to make use of excess basil, which is often a challenge for gardeners. This dish is simple and full of the bright flavor of that popular summertime crop. A pasta side dish such as Egg Noodles with Tomato (page 177) is a perfect match with the pesto; Mashed White Beans and Garlic (page 182) is also good.

1½ pounds raw large shrimp (about 48), peeled and deveined
1½ cups packed fresh basil leaves
¼ cup almonds (any style)
1 large garlic clove
¼ cup olive oil
1 tablespoon fresh lemon juice
salt
freshly ground black pepper
crusty bread

Preheat the oven to 450°F.

Arrange the shrimp in a shallow baking dish just large enough to hold them in one layer, or divide evenly among four individual baking dishes.

Combine the remaining ingredients (except bread) in a blender and blend until smooth. Pour the pesto over the shrimp.

Bake 10 to 12 minutes or until shrimp are just firm. Serve the shrimp with crusty bread.

NOTE: This dish can be assembled up to 8 hours ahead of time. Combine the shrimp and pesto in a dish as directed and keep covered and refrigerated until ready to bake.

Serves 4

tsatsiki shrimp salad

Tsatsiki is a salad condiment used throughout Greece and often served in the United States as an accompaniment to gyros. Low-fat yogurt is okay to use, but nonfat yogurt produces a chalky, insipid sauce, hardly worth the savings in calories. This makes a pleasing hors d'oeuvre served with Pita Sticks (page 208).

2 cups minced, peeled, seeded cucumber (about 1½ cucumbers)
1 teaspoon salt
1 cup plain yogurt
2 garlic cloves, minced
2 tablespoons extra-virgin olive oil
2 tablespoons chopped fresh dill
1½ pounds peeled Simply Boiled Shrimp (page 2)
freshly ground black pepper

In a sieve, toss the cucumber with salt, and let it drain for one hour. Press out as much liquid as possible. Squeeze the cucumber dry in paper towels, then transfer to a bowl.

Stir in the remaining ingredients. The salad is best served immediately, but it can be kept covered and chilled for up to 24 hours. Stir it well if it becomes watery.

Serves 4 as a main course or 8 as an appetizer

roasted shrimp, potatoes, and prosciutto portuguese-style

Seafood and ham are often combined in Portuguese cuisine. Here, salty prosciutto, crispy potatoes, and briny shrimp unite in a satisfying, hearty one-dish meal.

¼ cup olive oil

1½ pounds all-purpose potatoes, peeled and cut into ½-inch cubes (about 3½ cups)

3 ounces thinly sliced prosciutto, cut into bite-size pieces

1 garlic clove, minced

¼ to ½ teaspoon hot red pepper flakes

½ teaspoon salt

1½ pounds raw large shrimp, peeled

⅓ cup dry white wine

½ cup chopped fresh coriander or parsley

Preheat the oven to 400°F.

Heat the oil in a large ovenproof nonstick skillet over moderately high heat and add the potatoes. Fry them, stirring, for about 10 minutes or until golden. Remove the pan from the heat and stir in the prosciutto, garlic, pepper flakes, and salt. Add the shrimp and toss to combine. Pour in the wine.

Bake 13 to 18 minutes or until the shrimp are firm and just cooked through. Stir in the coriander and serve immediately.

Serves 4

shrimp stuffed with pita, spinach, sun-dried tomatoes, and almonds

Stuffing individual shrimp can be very time consuming, especially if you are using small shrimp. Here is a way to serve stuffed shrimp for a large group without using all your time and money. The stuffing is equally suited for filling individual jumbo shrimp (see note). Serve with Zesty Asparagus (page 192) and a green salad.

1 cup chopped onion

2 garlic cloves, minced

2 tablespoons olive oil

2 tablespoons butter

¼ cup chopped almonds

2 teaspoons fennel seeds

3 cups coarsely ground fresh pita bread crumbs (about three 6-inch rounds)

1 10-ounce package frozen chopped spinach, defrosted

½ cup sun-dried tomatoes packed in oil, drained and chopped medium-fine

½ cup freshly grated Parmesan cheese

salt

freshly ground black pepper

1½ pounds raw medium to large shrimp, peeled

⅓ cup dry white wine

Preheat the oven to 350°F.

In a skillet, cook the onion and garlic in the oil and butter over moderate heat, stirring, until softened, about 5 minutes. Add the almonds and fennel seeds and cook for 5 to 10 minutes or until the mixture begins to turn golden. Add the pita crumbs and cook, stirring, for 5 minutes.

By handfuls, squeeze out excess water from the spinach and add to the skillet with the sun-dried tomatoes and Parmesan. Combine well and season with salt and pepper.

Butterfly the shrimp by halving them lengthwise through the rounded side without cutting all the way through, so they can be opened.

In a large baking dish (9-by-13-inch or equivalent), arrange half the shrimp, spread open with cut sides up. Top the shrimp with the stuffing mixture, pressing it down slightly, and arrange the remaining shrimp on top, spread open with cut sides down. Drizzle the wine on top and cover the dish with foil.

Bake for 15 to 20 minutes or until the shrimp are cooked through.

NOTE: This can be prepared 1 day in advance, before baking. Make sure the stuffing is cooled completely before assembling. Keep it covered in the refrigerator until ready to cook.

To stuff individual jumbo shrimp, press a large spoonful of the filling onto the cut side of each shrimp, enclosing it slightly. Bake the shrimp in a single layer, stuffing side up.

Serves 6

shrimp and sausage jambalaya

This dish was born from a recipe my friend Sallie from Louisiana shared with me. Depending on your taste and time, other ingredients can be added, such as chicken, tomatoes, clams, and herbs. However you make it, this is bayou comfort food at its best! Serve with a tossed salad and you've got a meal.

1 pound smoked sausage, such as kielbasa or hot links, sliced ¼ inch thick

6 or 7 scallions, trimmed

1 large green bell pepper, chopped

2 celery ribs, chopped

3 large garlic cloves, chopped

3 cups chicken broth

1½ cups uncooked long-grain rice

½ teaspoon dried thyme

1 pound raw small to large shrimp, peeled

freshly ground black pepper

In a large heavy saucepan, cook the sausage over moderate heat until browned. With a slotted spoon, transfer the sausage to a plate.

Chop the scallions, reserving the dark green parts for garnish; add the white and pale green parts to the saucepan. Add the green pepper, celery, and garlic. Cook over moderate heat, stirring, for 5 minutes. Add the broth, rice, thyme, and reserved sausage. Bring the mixture to a boil. Reduce the heat to a simmer and cook the jamba–laya, covered, for 10 minutes. Stir in the shrimp and pepper and cook the mixture, covered, for 10 to 15 minutes more or until the shrimp are just done and the rice is tender.

Serve the jambalaya sprinkled with the reserved scallion greens.

NOTE: You don't need to add salt, as it is provided by the canned broth and sausage.

Serves 4 to 6

shrimp in greek tomato herb and feta sauce

There is something about the briny, tangy, creamy, classic Greek combination of shrimp and feta that is enticing. Put it on top of another universal favorite, pasta, and you've got a winner. A salad and some bread are all the extras needed for a complete spread.

1 cup water

1 bay leaf

1 teaspoon salt

2 pounds raw small to large shrimp

1 large garlic clove, minced

1 tablespoon olive oil

½ cup chopped fresh parsley leaves

2 tablespoons chopped fresh mint leaves

½ teaspoon hot red pepper flakes

½ teaspoon dried oregano

1 1-pound can whole tomatoes, drained, chopped, and drained again

4 ounces feta cheese

salt

freshly ground black pepper

¾ pound dried pasta, cooked, or 4½ cups cooked rice (1½ cups uncooked) as an accompaniment

In a large saucepan, bring the water to a boil with bay leaf and salt. Add the shrimp and boil for 2 minutes, stirring. Drain the shrimp in a colander set over a bowl, reserving the cooking liquid. Rinse the shrimp quickly under cold water and peel them.

In a large deep skillet, cook the garlic in the oil over moderate heat, stirring, for 2 minutes. Add the reserved cooking liquid, parsley, mint, pepper flakes, oregano, and tomatoes. Simmer the sauce, stirring, for 5 minutes.

Rinse the feta well under cold water and cut into ½-inch dice. Stir the shrimp into the hot sauce and heat until sauce just simmers. Remove the pan from heat and gently stir in the feta, seasoning with salt and pepper. Serve over pasta or rice.

NOTE: The sauce and shrimp can be prepared 1 day in advance, kept separately covered and refrigerated. Reheat the sauce to continue.

Serves 4

shrimp and artichoke fettuccine alfredo

This dish, though comforting and unassuming, is also elegant and sumptuous. Served as a first course, your guests will think you've knocked yourself out. There is no need for them to know how simple it really is. For a complete meal, round out this satisfying pasta with Watercress and Butter with Balsamic Vinegar (page 193), Braised Escarole with Tomatoes and Garlic (page 184) or Green Salad with Grapes and Walnuts (page 205).

12 ounces dried fettucine

1 large garlic clove, minced

2 tablespoons olive oil

1 14-ounce can artichoke hearts (7 or 8 small hearts), drained and quartered

1 pound small to medium shrimp, peeled and halved lengthwise

1¼ cups half-and-half (see Note)

2 large eggs

½ cup freshly grated Parmesan cheese

salt

freshly ground black pepper

minced fresh parsley (optional)

In a large kettle of boiling salted water cook the fettucini until tender.

While the pasta is cooking, cook the garlic in the oil in a large deep skillet over moderate heat, stirring, for 1 minute. Add the artichokes and cook, stirring, for 2 minutes. Add the shrimp and cook, stirring, for 2 to 3 minutes or until the shrimp are almost cooked through.

Whisk together the half-and-half and eggs. Drain the fettucine, but do not rinse. Add the hot pasta to the skillet and pour the egg mixture on top. Stir and toss the pasta over low heat until the sauce thickens. (Do not overheat or the sauce could curdle). Stir in the Parmesan and salt and pepper and serve immediately. Garnish with the parsley if desired.

NOTE: Skim or low-fat milk can be substituted for the half-and-half, but be even more careful not to boil the sauce, because lower-fat milk will curdle more quickly.

Serves 4 as a main course or 6 as an appetizer

shrimp with broccoli rabe, bacon, and pasta

Boiling the broccoli rabe removes some of the bitterness, allowing its lovely "green" flavor to shine through in this hearty one-dish meal.

1½ pounds broccoli rabe, trimmed and washed well (see Note)
½ pound dried thin spaghetti
6 slices lean bacon
3 tablespoons olive oil
1½ cups thinly sliced onion
2 garlic cloves, minced
1½ pounds raw peeled shrimp
¼ cup white wine
¼ to ½ teaspoon hot red pepper flakes
½ cup water
1 14- or 16-ounce can whole peeled tomatoes, drained well and chopped
salt
freshly ground black pepper

In a large pot of boiling salted water, cook the broccoli rabe for 3 to 5 minutes or until it is crisp, tender, but not soft. Remove the greens with a slotted spoon or sieve. Drain and coarsely chop.

In the same pot of boiling water, cook the spaghetti until just tender, drain, and rinse briefly.

Cut the bacon crosswise into thin strips. In a heavy skillet, cook it over moderate heat until crisp. Transfer bacon to a plate with a slotted spoon.

Pour off all but 1 tablespoon bacon fat from the skillet and add the olive oil, onion, and garlic. Cook over moderate heat, stirring, until softened and beginning to brown. Add the shrimp and wine and cook, stirring, for 5 minutes. Add the broccoli rabe, pepper flakes, water, and tomatoes and bring to a boil. Stir in the bacon and pasta and season with salt and pepper. Serve immediately

NOTE: Other greens, such as kale, beet greens, Swiss chard, spinach, and even regular broccoli can be substituted for the broccoli rabe. But be careful when blanching the greens, and taste at intervals, as the cooking time varies greatly with the tenderness of the vegetable.

Serves 4

simply spiced shrimp

Cooking doesn't get much easier than this, but it still took me a while to catch on. Being a northerner, I didn't realize that everyone south of Baltimore knows spiced shrimp like New Englanders know maple syrup. I tried spicing up my shrimp and crabs with a spice mix called "Shrimp and Crab Boil." I took the cue from the name and added the spices to boiling water to boil the shellfish. Not until I moved to Maryland crab country did I find out that you douse the shellfish with spices and steam them *over* boiling water. Perhaps someone should market a spice mix called "Shrimp and Crab Steam" for us literalists.

The shrimp are cooked with their shells on, so provide lots of napkins for spice-coated hands and beer or lemonade for spice-coated throats.

2 pounds raw medium shrimp, shells left on

¼ cup "shrimp and crab boil" spices such as Old Bay Seasoning (see Note)

lemon wedges

Set an expandable steaming basket (use one with legs) in a pot and add water until it just touches the bottom of the basket. Cover the kettle and bring water to a rolling boil. Add the shrimp and sprinkle with the spices. Steam the shrimp, covered tightly, for 5 minutes or until firm and just cooked through.

Serve the shrimp with lemon wedges and a dish of the spices for dipping if desired.

NOTE: If you can't find a prepared spice mix you can make your own.

BLEND TOGETHER:

  1 tablespoon chili powder

  1 tablespoon paprika

  ¼ teaspoon cayenne pepper

  1 finely ground bay leaf

  ½ teaspoon dry mustard

  1 teaspoon dried oregano

  1 teaspoon salt

  ½ teaspoon black pepper

  1 teaspoon sugar

  ½ teaspoon ground coriander seed

Serves 4

curried shrimp with sweet onions

This dish is equally good served hot over rice or chilled on a bed of lettuce (a nice way to enjoy leftovers).

1 sweet onion (such as Vidalia), sliced (about 2 cups)
1 teaspoon vegetable oil
1½ teaspoons curry powder
2 tablespoons lemon juice or raspberry vinegar
¼ cup water
2 pounds raw medium shrimp, peeled
salt
freshly ground black pepper
3 cups cooked rice or lettuce leaves as an accompaniment
chopped basil and/or coriander

In a large nonstick skillet, cook the onion in oil over moderate heat, stirring, until tender but still slightly crisp. Stir in the curry powder and cook, stirring, for 1 minute. Add the lemon juice, water, and shrimp and simmer for 5 minutes or until shrimp are cooked through. Season with salt and pepper.

Serve hot over rice or chilled on a bed of lettuce. Both can be sprinkled with the herbs.

Serves 4

cornmeal fried shrimp

Go for a completely southern menu and serve with Herbed Parmesan Grits (page 174) and Collard Greens with a Northern Accent (page 204).

2 large eggs
¼ cup cornstarch
¼ cup yellow cornmeal
2 pounds raw large shrimp, peeled and deveined
vegetable oil for frying
coarse sea or kosher salt
Fresh Tomato Salsa (page 207) or bottled salsa

In a shallow dish, beat the eggs lightly. Put the cornstarch and cornmeal in separate dishes. Dip each shrimp in cornstarch, then egg, then cornmeal.

In a large deep skillet, heat ¼ inch of oil over moderately high heat until it is very hot, but not smoking. Add some of the shrimp to the skillet, leaving plenty of room between them, and fry them for 1 to 2 minutes on each side until they are crisp and cooked through. Transfer the shrimp to brown paper to drain and sprinkle them with salt. Fry the remaining shrimp.

Serve the shrimp immediately with the salsa.

Serves 8 as an appetizer or 4 as a main course

deviled shrimp

Something is "deviled" when it is spiced up with hot pepper or mustard. When raw shrimp are halved lengthwise, they curl and twist into corkscrew shapes when cooked. Serve these devilish, twisted shrimp with cut-up melon and a nice crusty bread to make a perfect luncheon or light supper dish.

2 pounds raw small-to-large shrimp

1½ tablespoons Dijon mustard

2 tablespoons mayonnaise

1 tablespoon sweet pickle relish

2 tablespoons drained capers

1 tablespoon fresh lemon juice

¼ cup olive or vegetable oil

½ cup chopped red onion

1 red, yellow, or orange bell pepper, sliced thin

salt

freshly ground black pepper

8 large lettuce leaves, washed and spun dry

Peel the shrimp and halve them lengthwise. Bring a saucepan of salted water to a boil, add the shrimp, and boil 3 minutes or until cooked through. Drain and rinse briefly under cold water to stop the cooking.

In a bowl whisk together the mustard, mayonnaise, relish, capers, and lemon juice until combined well. Whisk in the oil until the dressing is emulsified. Add the shrimp, onion, bell pepper, salt, and pepper; toss well. Serve the shrimp on a bed of lettuce.

NOTE: If you are short on time, buy peeled, precooked shrimp and halve them lengthwise. All that is left is tossing and serving.

The dish can be prepared completely and kept refrigerated and covered for up to 2 days.

Serves 4

crisp sesame shrimp

If you love the taste of fried shrimp, but don't love to deep-fry, pan-frying is a great option. Sweet-and-Sour Noodle and Cabbage Slaw (page 200) or Gingered Spaghetti Squash (page 196) complement these irresistible shrimp.

2 pounds raw large shrimp, peeled
¼ cup finely crushed Saltine crackers
¼ cup sesame seeds (see Note)
¼ teaspoon freshly ground black pepper
vegetable oil for frying
bottled duck sauce as an accompaniment

Butterfly the shrimp by halving them lengthwise through the rounded side without cutting all the way through, but enough so that they can be opened.

In a shallow dish, combine the cracker crumbs, sesame seeds, and pepper. Dredge each shrimp in the crumb mixture.

In a large deep skillet, heat ¼ inch of oil over moderately high heat until it is very hot, but not smoking. Add some of the shrimp to the skillet, leaving plenty of room between each, and fry them for 1 to 2 minutes on each side until they are crisp and cooked through. Transfer the shrimp to brown paper to drain and fry the remaining shrimp.

Serve immediately with duck sauce.

NOTE: Sesame seeds have a high fat content and therefore go rancid easily. I keep a well-sealed glass bottle in the freezer, but make sure they are fresh to start with, or they can ruin a dish.

Serves 8 as an appetizer or 4 as a main course

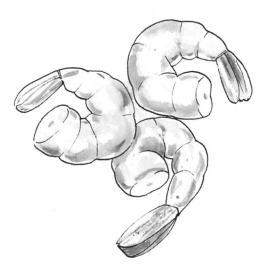

crisp coconut graham shrimp

The combination of the two sweet coatings, coconut and graham crackers, produces an irresistible crisp, lightly caramelized crust. If serving this shrimp as a main dish, accompany it with Gingered Spaghetti Squash (page 196) or Sweet-and-Sour Noodle Cabbage Slaw (page 200).

½ cup sweetened flaked coconut

½ cup graham cracker crumbs

⅓ cup all-purpose flour

½ teaspoon baking powder

½ teaspoon salt

½ teaspoon freshly ground black pepper

½ cup seltzer or club soda

1 large egg

vegetable oil for deep-frying

1½ pounds raw shrimp (medium to extra large), peeled and split down the back

Sweet, Hot, and Sour Chutney Sauce (recipe follows)

In a food processor, grind together the coconut and graham cracker crumbs. Transfer to a shallow dish.

Whisk together the flour, baking powder, salt, pepper, seltzer, and egg until just smooth.

In a large pot, heat 2 inches of oil to 360°F (use a deep-fat thermometer). Working with 4 to 6 shrimp at a time, dip each in the batter, letting the excess drip off. Then dredge in the coconut/graham mixture. After the shrimp are coated, drop them into the oil and fry for 3 to 5 minutes or until golden. Cut into the first shrimp to make sure it is cooked through. Drain the shrimp on brown paper and keep warm, uncovered, in a warm oven. Continue frying the remaining shrimp, letting the oil return to 360°F between batches.

Serve the shrimp with the sauce.

Serves 6 as an appetizer or 4 as a main course

sweet, hot, and sour chutney sauce

3 tablespoons Major Grey's mango chutney
2 tablespoons fresh lime or lemon juice
¼ teaspoon Tabasco
1 teaspoon soy sauce

Chop the solids in the chutney to a paste and whisk together all the ingredients.

NOTE: Covered and refrigerated, the sauce keeps for up to 1 week.

Makes about ⅓ cup

shrimp pot pie

Just as chicken pot pie stretches a small amount of chicken, this is a way to make a meal out of a few shrimp. This truly is a meal in a dish, complete with vegetables and bread.

1 medium onion, chopped

3 tablespoons butter

1 cup sliced carrots

1 cup sliced celery, including some leaves

½ cup all-purpose flour

1¾ cup chicken broth

¾ cup milk

1 bay leaf

1 teaspoon paprika

1 pound raw small-to-large shrimp, peeled

1 cup frozen peas

2 teaspoons fresh lemon juice

2 teaspoons Worcestershire sauce

salt

freshly ground black pepper

1 frozen pie-dough round, or ½ package frozen puff pastry, thawed

Preheat oven to 400°F.

In a large skillet, cook the onion in butter over moderate heat, stirring until softened. Add the carrots and celery and cook for one minute. Add the flour and cook the mixture, stirring until all of the flour is moistened. Add the broth, milk, bay leaf, and paprika and simmer the mixture, stirring constantly, for 5 minutes. Remove the pan from the heat and stir in the shrimp, peas, lemon juice, Worcestershire, salt, and pepper. Transfer the mixture to a 2-quart baking dish.

Roll out the dough, large enough to cover the dish and drape it over the top. Press the dough to the edge of the dish and trim off any excess.

Bake the pie for 35 minutes or until the crust is crisp and golden brown. Spoon out the pie, serving a piece of crust with each portion.

NOTE: The pie filling can be prepared up to 6 hours in advance. Keep covered and refrigerated in the baking dish. Top with the dough just before baking.

Serves 4

salmon

Sesame-Crusted Salmon Teriyaki

Jerk-Spiced Salmon Steaks

Crispy Salmon on Tangerine and Bacon Spinach

Grilled Molasses Salmon with Lime

Peppered Salmon

Grilled Salmon Steaks on Citrus

Grilled Salmon with Green Chili Coconut Sauce

Salmon in Green Chili Cream

Sautéed Salmon with Asparagus and Chickpea Vinaigrette

Blackened Salmon on Zesty Cabbage

Slow-Fried Herbed Salmon in Extra-Virgin Olive Oil

Crisp Salmon on Lentils with Fried Onions

Sautéed Salmon Smothered in Summer (Tomatoes and Basil)

Baked Salmon with Bell Pepper Salsa

Roasted Salmon Puttanesca (Tomato, Olive, and Caper Sauce)

Salmon-Stuffed Portobello Mushroom Caps

Salmon Pie with Roasted Peppers, Leeks, and Horseradish

Salmon Roasted in Garlic Butter

Salmon Baked with Apricots and Water Chestnuts

Salmon Baked with Deviled-Egg Sauce

Salmon and Fennel Under Wraps

Salmon Poached in Sake with Ginger and Celery

Simply Poached Salmon

Salmon Poached in Lemon Tomato Broth

Salmon in Grape Sauce

Salmon in Mock Tamarind Sauce

Salmon Cobb Salad with Creamy Mustard Dressing

Asian-Style Salmon Lettuce Rolls

Seared Salmon with Mesclun and Raspberry Vermouth Vinaigrette

Poached Salmon with Cucumber-Yogurt Sauce

Salmon and Yellow Pepper Chowder

sesame-crusted salmon teriyaki

Asian flavors, with their sweet, salty, and acidic clean tastes, complement salmon beautifully. Serve this with Sweet-and-Sour Noodle and Cabbage Slaw (page 200), Cauliflower with Caramelized Onions and Poppy Seeds (page 185), or Sautéed Fennel and Apples (page 189).

½ cup light soy sauce
½ cup mirin (see Note)
4 salmon steaks (about 8 ounces each)
½ cup sesame seeds
coarse sea or kosher salt
freshly ground black pepper

In a large plastic bag, combine the soy sauce and mirin. Add the salmon, coating it well with the marinade, and seal the bag. Let the salmon marinate, chilled, for at least 1 hour and up to 6 hours.

Remove the salmon from the bag and discard the marinade. Spread the sesame seeds on a plate and season the salmon with salt and pepper, then coat both sides of each steak with the seeds, patting them on to adhere.

Preheat a grill, or broiler with rack in the top position.

Brush the grill with oil and grill the salmon (or broil it on a rack set in a baking pan) for 6 minutes on each side or until just cooked through.

NOTE: Mirin is a syrupy Japanese rice wine. It is available in Asian markets, but I have also found it in the international sections of supermarkets, made by Kikkoman. If you can't find it, you can substitute ¼ cup sugar or corn syrup and 1 tablespoon lemon juice.

This marinade works well for any fish steaks, including swordfish, halibut, and tuna.

Serves 4

jerk-spiced salmon steaks

If you've ever tasted genuine "jerk" anything—that is, something (usually chicken) seasoned with a fiery hot blend of Jamaican allspice, Scotch bonnet peppers, scallions, and many other flavors and grilled over an open fire—then you'll recognize the kick in this dish. Beware! This is not for the dainty-palated. Broiled Ripe Plantains (page 194) are a good foil to the spicy heat.

4 scallions, trimmed to 4-inch lengths

1 Scotch bonnet, Habanero, or jalapeño chili,
   including the seeds but with stem removed (see Note)

¼ teaspoon ground allspice

⅛ teaspoon ground nutmeg

¼ teaspoon dried thyme

1 teaspoon sugar

1 teaspoon salt

½ teaspoon freshly ground black pepper

2 teaspoons vinegar, lime juice, or lemon juice

1 tablespoon water

4 salmon steaks (about 8 ounces each)

lime or lemon wedges

In a food processor or blender, puree all of the ingredients except the salmon and citrus wedges, scraping down the sides often.

Put the salmon in a dish. Using a spoon or spatula, spread it on all sides with the puree. Let the salmon marinate, covered and chilled, for 30 minutes to 4 hours.

Preheat a grill, or broiler with rack in the top position.

Brush the preheated grill with oil and grill the salmon (or broil it on a rack set in a baking pan) 6 minutes on each side or until just cooked through. Serve the salmon with lime or lemon wedges.

NOTE: Wear rubber gloves when handling, seeding, and chopping hot chilis. If you have ever handled a moderately hot chili (such as a jalapeño) and then touched your eye or mouth, you know the results can be irritating. Scotch bonnet and Habanero chilis are *much* hotter, and you can get seriously hurt if you do not heed this warning.

Jerk shrimp are delicious as well.

Serves 4

crispy salmon on tangerine and bacon spinach

As an article in the *Washington Post* once said, and I know many who agree, "there is no food that can't be improved by the addition of bacon or chocolate." Although this salmon tastes pretty good on the tangerine spinach alone, the extra salty crunch of the bacon adds the exclamation point. Serve this with Mashed White Beans and Garlic (page 182) or Skinny Scalloped Potatoes (page 172).

1 pound fresh spinach, coarse stems
    discarded and leaves washed well

4 slices bacon, cut crosswise into thin strips

1½ pounds center-cut salmon fillet, skinned
    and cut crosswise into 4 portions

coarse kosher or sea salt

freshly ground black pepper

½ cup fresh squeezed tangerine juice (see Note)

⅛ teaspoon freshly grated nutmeg

In a salad spinner or with paper towels, dry the spinach.

In a large nonstick skillet, cook the bacon over moderate heat, stirring, until crisp. Transfer the bacon with a slotted spoon to paper to drain. Pour off all but 1 tablespoon of the bacon fat.

Season the salmon on all sides with salt and pepper. Heat the remaining bacon fat in the skillet over moderate heat and sauté the salmon, skinned side up, for 4 to 5 minutes. Turn the salmon and cook 4 to 5 minutes more. Transfer the salmon to a plate and pour off the excess fat. Add the tangerine juice to the skillet and immediately add the spinach. Cook over moderate heat, stirring, until the spinach is just wilted. Season with nutmeg, salt, and pepper. Add the reserved bacon and return the salmon to the skillet. Simmer the mixture just until the salmon is reheated.

NOTE: If fresh tangerines are not available, some supermarkets carry frozen tangerine juice concentrate, which can be used after reconstituting. If that is not available, fresh orange juice can be substituted.

Serves 4

grilled molasses salmon
with lime

Round out this Caribbean-inspired dish with Quick Rice and Beans (page 178), Broiled Ripe Plantains (page 194), and a salad.

FOR MARINADE

3 tablespoons dark molasses

1 tablespoon fresh lime juice

1 tablespoon vegetable oil plus additional for brushing grill

4 salmon steaks (about 8 ounces each)

coarse kosher or sea salt

freshly ground black pepper

lime wedges as an accompaniment

In a small bowl, whisk together the marinade ingredients.

Put the salmon in a shallow dish or plastic bag and pour the marinade over it, coating the salmon well. Let it marinate, covered and refrigerated, for 1 to 4 hours. Discard the marinade and season the salmon with salt and pepper.

Preheat a grill, or broiler with rack in the top position.

Brush the preheated grill with oil and grill the salmon (or broil it on a rack set in a baking pan) for 6 minutes on each side or until just cooked through. Serve the salmon with lime wedges.

NOTE: Halibut or swordfish can be substituted for the salmon.

Serves 4

peppered salmon

This is the first recipe that got me hooked on salmon. The pepper makes a delightful, not-too-spicy crust, which cuts the richness of the salmon. Serve something acidic with this to counteract the "heat," such as a salad with a basic vinaigrette, Zesty Asparagus (page 192), or Sweet-and-Sour Noodle and Cabbage Slaw (page 200).

3 tablespoons soy sauce

1 teaspoon sugar

1½ pounds center-cut salmon fillet, skinned and cut crosswise into 4 portions

2 tablespoons coarsely ground black pepper

½ teaspoon coarse kosher or sea salt

1 tablespoon vegetable oil

In a shallow dish or plastic bag, mix together the soy sauce and sugar, then add the salmon. Coat the salmon well and let it marinate, covered and refrigerated, for at least 1 hour and up to 8 hours.

Discard the marinade and pat the salmon dry with paper towels. Coat the salmon on all sides with the pepper, patting it on to help it adhere, and sprinkle with the salt.

Heat the oil in a large nonstick skillet over moderately high heat. Fry the salmon, skinned side up, in the skillet for 5 minutes. Turn the salmon and continue frying, reducing the heat to medium if the salmon is getting too dark, for 5 minutes or until it is just cooked through.

Serves 4

grilled salmon steaks on citrus

My neighbor Mark showed me his technique for keeping whole fish and fillets from sticking to the grill. Since sticking is less of a problem with fish steaks, here we rely on the citrus slices to lend a delicate flavor as they char. The sight of fish grilling on this bed of colorful fruit is impressive. The fruit insulates the fish from the heat, so the cooking time is longer. Try the Green Salad with Grapes and Walnuts (page 205) and Old Bay Seasoned Roasted New Potatoes (page 171) on the side.

1 grapefruit

1 orange

1 lime

1 lemon

5 to 7 large fresh basil branches with
    leaves attached

½ teaspoon salt

½ teaspoon pepper

4 salmon steaks (about 8 ounces each)

Slice half the grapefruit, half the orange, half the lime, and half the lemon into ¼-inch slices and reserve. Squeeze the juice from the remaining fruit halves into a bowl.

Remove the leaves from the basil and reserve the stems with the citrus slices. Mince the leaves and add to the juice with the salt and pepper.

Preheat a grill. When ready to cook, lay the citrus slices on the grill in a single layer, as close together as possible, and top with the basil stems. Season the salmon with salt and pepper and lay it on top of the fruit and stems. Cook for about 10 minutes on each side, basting often and generously with the basil citrus juice, or until the salmon is just cooked through. Discard the charred citrus slices.

NOTE: This is an excellent way to grill any fish.

Serves 4

grilled salmon with green chili coconut sauce

Inspired by Thai green curry sauce, the complex flavors here blend with the salmon beautifully, first as a marinade, then as an accompanying sauce. Serve with Zesty Asparagus (page 192) and Egg Noodles with Tomato (page 177).

FOR THE SAUCE

1 cup canned unsweetened coconut milk (see Note)

zest of 1 lime, removed in strips with a vegetable peeler

1 anchovy filet

1 tablespoon chopped pickled jalapeños or 1 fresh
  seeded jalapeño (include some seeds if desired for extra heat)

½ cup firmly packed fresh basil leaves

½ cup firmly packed fresh cilantro sprigs (see Note)

½ teaspoon salt

4 salmon steaks (about 8 ounces each)

coarse kosher or sea salt

vegetable oil for brushing the grill

Combine all of the sauce ingredients in a blender and puree until smooth.

Place the salmon in a shallow dish and pour the sauce over it, coating the steaks well. Let them marinate, covered and refrigerated, for 10 minutes up to 8 hours.

Remove the salmon from the sauce, dragging the steaks across the edge of the dish to remove the excess sauce, and transfer the sauce to a small saucepan. Sprinkle the salmon lightly with salt.

Preheat a grill, or broiler with rack in the top position.

Brush the grill with oil and grill the salmon (or broil it on a rack set in a baking pan) for 6 minutes on each side or until just cooked through.

Bring the sauce to a boil and simmer gently, stirring, for 5 minutes. Spoon some of the sauce over the salmon and serve any remaining sauce separately.

NOTE: Canned, unsweetened Thai coconut milk is available in Asian markets and many supermarkets in the international or specialty foods section. If not, ask your grocer to order it for you. Beware: sweet cream of coconut is not a substitute.

Cilantro stems are more tender and flavorful than those of other herbs such as parsley and basil, so it is not necessary to separate every cilantro leaf from the stems. Discard the large coarse stems and use the tender sprigs, stem and all.

Serves 4

salmon in green chili cream

Moderately hot chilis add just the right bite to complement the silky sweet cream in this sauce. On the side, try Fried Corn and Peppers with Butter and Basil (page 191) and Toasted Vermicelli and Herbs (page 137).

3 long hot green chilis, seeded and chopped (see Note)

1 medium onion, chopped

1 large garlic clove, minced

1 tablespoon vegetable oil

1 tablespoon fresh lemon juice

½ cup water

1½ pounds center-cut salmon fillet, skinned
    and cut crosswise into 4 portions, or 4 salmon steaks
    (about 8 ounces each)

coarse kosher or sea salt

freshly ground black pepper

½ cup heavy cream

In a large skillet, cook the chilis, onion, and garlic in the oil over moderately low heat, stirring, until the vegetables are tender and begin to turn golden. Reduce the heat to low and stir in the lemon juice and water. Season the salmon with salt and pepper and lay it on the vegetables. Cook, covered, for 8 to 10 minutes or until the salmon is barely cooked through.

Transfer the salmon to a plate. (Do not worry about some of the vegetables clinging to the salmon.) Transfer the mixture left in the skillet to a blender or food processor. Add the cream and puree until smooth. Return the sauce to the skillet. Season with salt and pepper and add the salmon. Heat the sauce and the salmon over moderate heat, shaking the skillet, until the salmon is heated through.

NOTE: Fresh chilis are available across the country in vast and confusing varieties. This recipe calls for "long hot green," which can refer to a number of different types. If you are confused, ask the produce manager at your supermarket. For this recipe you want green chilis about 1 inch in diameter around the stem and 4 to 8 inches long. It can be curled or straight, Anaheim or "long hot green." As long as they are medium hot and not killer hot they will work. You still need to wear rubber gloves when handling medium hot chilis, especially the seeds!

sautéed salmon with asparagus and chickpea vinaigrette

When we are in Vermont, the only quality fish I can be sure to get are shrimp, salmon, and swordfish. I thought fresh salmon would be a treat for a friend from the coast of South Africa, who is used to plenty of fresh fish but had not had any since his move to Vermont. In my modest kitchen in the north, I came up with this version of crisp sautéed salmon using a dash of dark Vermont maple syrup. After one bite he looked up at me with a shocked look and said quietly, "This is the best fish I have ever tasted." The combination of vegetables, acidic sauce, and rich, silky salmon combine to make this my favorite salmon dish.

½ pound asparagus, trimmed

¼ cup fresh lemon juice

½ cup olive oil plus 1 tablespoon
   for cooking salmon

1 tablespoon pure maple syrup or
   1 teaspoon honey

coarse kosher or sea salt

freshly ground black pepper

1 cup canned chickpeas, white beans,
   or black beans, rinsed well

3 tablespoons minced fresh chives or scallions

1½ pounds center-cut skinned salmon fillet,
   cut crosswise into 4 portions

Cut the asparagus into one-inch pieces at an angle. In a pot of boiling salted water, blanch the asparagus for 1 to 2 minutes or until tender but crisp. Drain and rinse briefly under cold water.

In a bowl, whisk together the lemon juice, ½ cup oil, the syrup, and salt and pepper. Stir the asparagus, chickpeas, and chives into the lemon mixture.

Season the salmon with salt and pepper. In a large nonstick skillet, heat 1 tablespoon oil over moderate heat and sauté the salmon for 5 to 7 minutes on each side or until crisp and cooked through. Add the asparagus mixture to the skillet just to warm the sauce. Divide the salmon and sauce among four plates and serve.

Serves 4

blackened salmon on zesty cabbage

This dish was inspired by a blackened redfish I tasted at the Commander's Palace restaurant in New Orleans. I have greatly reduced the amount of butter, but it still retains the creamy, tangy flavors I so enjoyed. Skinny Scalloped Potatoes (page 172) or Mashed White Beans and Garlic (page 182) makes a good side dish.

1 onion, sliced thin

3 tablespoons butter

1 teaspoon grated lemon zest

3 tablespoons fresh lemon juice

1 cup dry white wine such as sauvignon blanc, chenin blanc, or Chablis

1 teaspoon sugar

1 small head Napa cabbage, sliced thin crosswise (about 8 cups sliced) (see Note)

4 teaspoons chili powder

4 teaspoons sesame seeds

2 teaspoons salt

1 teaspoon black pepper

1 tablespoon vegetable oil

1½ pounds center-cut salmon fillet, skinned and cut crosswise into 4 portions

In a large skillet, cook the onion in the butter over moderate heat, stirring occasionally, until pale golden. Add the lemon zest, juice, wine, and sugar and cook over moderately high heat until liquid is reduced by half, about 15 minutes. Add the cabbage and cook, stirring, until it is wilted and just tender. Add salt and pepper to taste and keep warm while the salmon is cooking.

In a small bowl, combine chili powder, sesame seeds, salt, and pepper. Coat the salmon with the mixture. Heat 1 tablespoon of oil in a large nonstick skillet over moderately high heat and add the salmon. If the salmon is browning too quickly, reduce the heat to moderate. Cook for four to five minutes on each side or until brown and crisp (blackened does not mean burned) and just cooked through.

Divide the cabbage among four plates and top with the salmon.

NOTE: Napa cabbage is a delicate, curly-leafed cabbage. It has a tightly packed, elongated head, with curly pale green to yellow leaves on white ribs. The cabbage can be simply sliced crosswise starting at the top of the head, to make shreds. Regular cabbage can be substituted, but it may take longer cooking time to become tender.

Serves 4

slow-fried herbed salmon in extra-virgin olive oil

The herbs in the recipe are just suggestions; other fresh herbs, such as chives, tarragon, sage, oregano, cilantro, and mint, can be substituted. Taste your herbs first to adjust the amounts to their strength of flavor. Frying the salmon over a low temperature allows the outside to get crispy without burning the herbs, while the inside cooks slowly to moist perfection. Possible side dishes are Egg Noodles with Tomato (page 177), Zucchini Casserole (page 198), or Braised Escarole with Tomatoes and Garlic (page 184).

1½ pounds center-cut salmon fillet, skinned and cut crosswise into 4 portions

2 tablespoons extra-virgin olive oil

⅓ cup finely chopped fresh parsley

2 tablespoons minced fresh dill

1 teaspoon minced fresh thyme leaves

coarse kosher or sea salt

freshly ground black pepper

Arrange the salmon on a platter and rub all over with 1 tablespoon of oil.

In a small bowl, combine the herbs. Coat the salmon on all sides with the mixture. The salmon can be cooked immediately or kept covered and refrigerated for up to 8 hours.

Heat the remaining tablespoon of olive oil in a large nonstick skillet over moderately low heat. Season the salmon with salt and pepper and cook it in the skillet for 8 to 10 minutes on each side or until slightly crispy and just cooked through.

Serves 4

crisp salmon on lentils with fried onions

This delicious dish looks complicated and impressive, but is simple to prepare. Serve with Toasted Vermicelli and Herbs (page 176) or Blasted Vegetables (page 188) and a tossed salad on the side.

FOR THE LENTILS

1 cup brown or green lentils, rinsed

3 cups water

¼ cup olive oil

2 carrots, chopped

¼ teaspoon dried thyme

½ cup white wine

½ teaspoon salt

½ teaspoon freshly ground black pepper

1 tablespoon malt or wine vinegar

FOR THE ONIONS

2 onions, sliced thin

1 tablespoon cornstarch or flour

1 cup vegetable oil

1½ pounds center-cut salmon fillet, skinned and cut crosswise into 4 portions

coarse kosher or sea salt

freshly ground black pepper

1 tablespoon olive oil

In a large saucepan, combine all the ingredients for the lentils except the vinegar. Simmer, partially covered, for 40 to 50 minutes or until lentils are just tender and most of the liquid is absorbed. Add the vinegar and additional salt and pepper, if necessary, and simmer 5 minutes more.

Toss together the onions and cornstarch.

In a large deep skillet, heat the vegetable oil over moderately high heat until hot but not smoking and add half the onion mixture. Fry until golden brown and transfer to paper towels with a slotted spoon. Sprinkle the onions immediately with salt. Repeat with the remaining onions. Keep the onions in a warm oven, uncovered, up to 1½ hours.

Season the salmon with salt and pepper. Heat the olive oil in a large nonstick skillet over moderate heat and add the salmon. Cook for 5 to 7 minutes on each side or until browned, crisp, and just cooked through.

Serve the salmon on a bed of the lentils, topped with the onions.

NOTE: The lentils can be prepared 1 day in advance. Keep covered in the refrigerator and reheat before serving.

Serves 4

sautéed salmon smothered in summer (tomatoes and basil)

This dish is my latest favorite "taste of summer" meal. It is simple. It lets the flavors shine. It is healthy. It can be made ahead and served warm or at room temperature. And you'll want to make extra to enjoy an instant salmon salad straight from the fridge the next day. What more could we ask? Round out the meal with Zesty Asparagus (page 192) and rice or crusty bread.

1 large vine-ripe tomato

½ cup finely chopped fresh basil leaves

1 tablespoon fresh lemon juice

1 tablespoon plus 1 teaspoon olive oil

1 whole 1½-to-2-pound piece of center-cut salmon fillet, skinned

coarse kosher or sea salt

freshly ground black pepper

Dice the tomato and transfer it with all its juices to a bowl. Add the basil, lemon, and 1 tablespoon olive oil and combine well. Let the sauce sit while preparing the salmon.

With a sharp knife, make three slashes across the salmon, cutting halfway through, to divide it into four portions but leaving the whole piece intact. Season the salmon with salt and pepper.

In a nonstick skillet, heat the remaining teaspoon of olive oil over moderately high heat until it is hot but not smoking. In it, sauté the salmon, slashed side down, for 5 minutes. Using two spatulas, turn the salmon and sauté for 5 to 7 minutes more or until just cooked through.

Slide the salmon onto a platter, slashed side up, and smother with the tomato mixture. Let the salmon stand for at least 10 minutes to absorb some of the juices before serving. The salmon can stand at room temperature for up to 45 minutes, or it can be refrigerated for up to 24 hours.

Serves 4

baked salmon with bell pepper salsa

The salsa is baked with the salmon to mix the fresh flavors into a sumptuous entrée. Serve with Skinny Scalloped Potatoes (page 172) or Herbed Parmesan Grits (page 174).

FOR THE SALSA

2½ cups diced red, yellow, and green bell peppers

2 tablespoons drained capers

½ teaspoon minced garlic

2 tablespoons olive oil

3 tablespoons chopped fresh basil leaves

1½ tablespoons red wine vinegar

4 salmon steaks (about 8 ounces each) or
   1½ pounds center-cut salmon fillet

coarse kosher or sea salt

freshly ground black pepper

Preheat oven to 400°F.

In a bowl, toss together the salsa ingredients.

Season the salmon with salt and pepper and arrange in a single layer in a baking dish. Pour the salsa on top and bake for 10 to 20 minutes or until just cooked through.

Serves 4

roasted salmon puttanesca (tomato, olive, and caper sauce)

Puttanesca is a quick, savory, and spicy Italian pasta sauce that enhances salmon beautifully. Serve with Blasted Sweet Potatoes with Salt, Malt Vinegar, and Parsley (page 170), or Toasted Vermicelli and Herbs (page 176).

FOR THE SAUCE

1 14- to 16-ounce can stewed tomatoes

⅔ cup pitted California black olives, chopped

3 tablespoons drained capers

2 cloves garlic, minced

½ teaspoon dried thyme

1 bay leaf

¼ teaspoon dried hot red pepper flakes, or to taste

4 salmon steaks (about 8 ounces each) or
　1½ pounds of salmon fillet

coarse kosher or sea salt

freshly ground black pepper

Preheat the oven to 400°F.

Combine the sauce ingredients in a saucepan and simmer the mixture, stirring, for 5 minutes.

Season the salmon with salt and pepper, and arrange in a single layer in a baking dish. Spoon the sauce around the salmon and bake for fifteen to twenty minutes or until just cooked through. Serve immediately.

Serves 4

salmon-stuffed portobello mushroom caps

These dressed-up salmon cakes make a great meal if you have company. They can be made ahead and are baked in one dish. The large juicy mushroom cap provides a meaty heartiness making Braised Escarole with Tomatoes and Garlic (page 184), or Toasted Vermicelli and Herbs (page 176) all that is needed for a robust menu.

1 pound salmon fillet, skinned

1 cup chopped onion

2 ribs celery, chopped

1 large garlic clove, minced

2 tablespoons vegetable or olive oil

½ cup dry white wine

1 tablespoon chopped fresh tarragon
  or 1 teaspoon dried

2 tablespoons mayonnaise

1 teaspoon salt

¼ teaspoon freshly ground black pepper

¼ cup minced fresh parsley, plus additional for garnish

4 large (about 4-inch diameter) Portabello mushrooms

¼ cup fresh bread crumbs

1½ tablespoons butter, cut into 4 thin pats

½ cup water

2 tablespoons fresh lemon juice

Preheat the oven to 350°F.

Feel the salmon with the fingertips to make sure there are no bones remaining. Cut the salmon into pieces and put in a food processor. Pulse the motor until the salmon is ground coarsely—do not puree. Transfer the salmon to a bowl.

In a small skillet, cook the onion, celery, and garlic in the oil over moderate heat, stirring, until softened. Add the wine and tarragon and boil the mixture until the liquid has evaporated. Stir the cooked vegetables, mayonnaise, salt, pepper, and parsley into the salmon.

With a damp towel, wipe the mushrooms clean and cut off the stems. Arrange the caps, stemmed ends up, in a large (9-by-13-inch) baking dish. Divide the salmon mixture among the caps, spreading it to the edges, and sprinkle the bread crumbs on top. Top each serving with a thin butter pat and pour the water and lemon juice around the caps into the dish.

Bake the mushrooms for 30 minutes or until the salmon is cooked through. Divide the mushrooms among four plates and sprinkle with parsley. Serve immediately.

NOTE: The mushrooms can be stuffed up to 6 hours in advance. Add the lemon juice and water just before baking.

Serves 4

salmon pie with roasted peppers, leeks, and horseradish

This version of salmon *en croute* is an easy way to encase salmon in an impressive puff pastry. For an elegant presentation, serve it with Green Salad with Grapes and Walnuts (page 205).

2 medium leeks, trimmed, washed well, and
   sliced thin (see Note)

2 tablespoons olive oil

1 14-ounce jar roasted red peppers, drained
   and coarsely chopped (about 1½ cups)

1 tablespoon bottled horseradish

coarse kosher or sea salt

freshly ground black pepper

1 pound frozen puff pastry, thawed

1½ pounds salmon fillet, skinned and cut into 4 pieces

Preheat the oven to 400°F.

In a large skillet, cook the leeks in the oil over moderate heat, stirring, for 5 minutes. Add the peppers and cook the mixture, stirring occasionally, for 15 to 20 minutes, until the mixture is as dry as possible without browning. Stir in the horseradish, salt, and pepper; let cool.

On a lightly floured surface, roll out half the dough and fit it into a 9-inch pie plate, leaving some overhang. Spread half the vegetable mixture in the bottom. Season the salmon with salt and pepper and arrange the pieces on top of the vegetables as evenly as possible. Top the salmon with the remaining vegetables. Brush the edge of the dough lightly with water.

Roll out the remaining dough until it is large enough to fit over the top with a generous overhang, and drape it over the pie. With scissors, trim the dough to within $\frac{1}{4}$ inch of the pie plate's rim. Pinch and tuck the edge of the dough under, sealing it with the back of a fork pressed against the rim. Cut out a $\frac{1}{2}$-inch hole in the top for a vent.

Bake the pie for 35 minutes or until golden brown. Let stand for 10 minutes before slicing.

NOTE: Leeks add a distinct delicate flavor, but a little grit can ruin an entire dish. Always wash them carefully. Trim the root ends and the tough dark green leaves. Split each leek lengthwise to within $\frac{1}{2}$ inch of the root end. With the leafy end hanging down, wash each leek under running water, separating each leaf to get out all of the dirt.

The pie can be assembled 8 hours in advance, kept uncovered and refrigerated.

Serves 6

salmon roasted in garlic butter

Shrimp scampi is known to many as an ideal Italian comfort food. Here, salmon gets the same treatment. You can't go wrong with garlic and butter, and a good crusty bread will sop up every rich drop. Serve with Old Bay Seasoned Roasted New Potatoes (page 171) or Egg Noodles with Tomato (page 177), and a tossed salad.

2 garlic cloves

¼ teaspoon salt

¼ teaspoon freshly ground black pepper

3 tablespoons butter

1½ pounds center-cut salmon fillet, skinned and cut crosswise into 4 portions

1 tablespoon fresh lemon juice

¼ cup minced fresh parsley

lemon wedges

Preheat oven to 400°F.

On a cutting board, with a fork, mash the garlic into a paste with the salt and pepper. Add the butter and mash into the garlic paste.

Arrange the salmon in a single layer in a baking dish. Top it with the garlic butter and drizzle with the lemon juice.

Bake for 10 to 15 minutes or until salmon is just cooked through. Sprinkle with the parsley and serve with lemon wedges.

Serves 4

salmon baked with apricots and water chestnuts

Moroccan and other cuisines of the Mediterranean and the East often combine meat and fish with fruits. The tartness of the apricots and lime and the crunch of the water chestnuts beautifully complement the richness of the salmon. Plain rice or couscous and Blasted Vegetables (page 188) make fine accompaniments.

butter for coating the dish

1½ pounds salmon fillet

⅓ cup chopped dried apricots

½ cup canned whole water chestnuts, drained, rinsed, and coarsely chopped

½ cup water

3 tablespoons fresh lime juice

1 tablespoon soy sauce

coarse kosher or sea salt

freshly ground black pepper

Preheat oven to 375°F. Butter a shallow baking dish large enough to hold the salmon in one layer.

Put the salmon in the prepared dish, skin side down.

In a medium saucepan, combine the remaining ingredients and simmer for 10 minutes. Pour on top of the salmon and bake for 10 to 20 minutes or until just cooked through.

Serve the salmon with its sauce spooned on top.

Serves 4

salmon baked with deviled-egg sauce

This retro dish makes a comforting meal any time of year. Serve with a simple tossed salad and Peas and Rye Croutons (page 190).

1 tablespoon butter

1 tablespoon drained capers

1 tablespoon all-purpose flour

⅔ cup milk (whole, skim, or low-fat)

½ cup chopped celery

2 teaspoons fresh lemon juice or vinegar

2 teaspoons Dijon mustard

coarse kosher or sea salt

freshly ground black pepper

2 hard-boiled eggs, chopped

¼ cup chopped red onion

1½ pounds skinned salmon fillet or 4 salmon steaks
(about 8 ounces each)

2 tablespoons minced fresh parsley

Preheat the oven to 400°F; set a rack in the upper third.

In a small saucepan, melt the butter with the capers over low heat. Add the flour and cook, stirring, for 2 minutes. Add the milk, whisking until smooth. Add the celery, lemon juice, mustard, salt, and pepper. Simmer the sauce, whisking, for 5 minutes. Remove the pan from the heat and stir in the eggs and onion.

Season the salmon with salt and pepper and put it in one layer in a baking dish. Spread the sauce on top of the salmon and bake it in the upper third of the oven for 20 to 30 minutes or until the salmon is just cooked through.

Sprinkle the salmon with the parsley before serving.

Serves 4

salmon and fennel under wraps

En papillote is the French term for baking something wrapped in parchment paper. Foil is a bit easier to work with and does essentially the same thing, sealing the food and allowing it to steam in its own juices. As accompaniments try Herbed Parmesan Grits (page 174) and Zesty Asparagus (page 192).

1 large fennel bulb

4 salmon steaks (about 8 ounces each) or fillets
  (about 6 ounces each)

1 teaspoon dried tarragon

1 teaspoon salt

freshly ground black pepper

Preheat oven to 350°F. Tear off four 12-inch sections of aluminum foil and lay them out flat.

Trim out the tough core from the bottom of the fennel bulb. Halve the bulb and slice it crosswise very thin. Reserve the feathery fennel tops. (They look like fresh dill.) Divide half of the sliced fennel among the sheets of foil. Put a salmon steak on top of each pile of fennel, and cover the salmon with the remaining fennel. Sprinkle each portion with the tarragon, salt, and pepper. Top each portion with a large sprig of fennel top.

Seal each foil package by bringing the sides together and crimping them securely. Put the packages on a baking sheet and bake for 20 to 25 minutes (about 5 minutes less for fillets), or until the salmon is just cooked through.

The salmon can be served in the foil, slit open, or transferred to a plate.

Serves 4

salmon poached in sake with ginger and celery

The delicate yet distinct flavors of sake, ginger, and celery combine to make this salmon dish one of the simplest and yet most sophisticated. Complement it with cooked medium-grain or sushi rice and Charred Soy and Sesame String Beans (page 183) or Zesty Asparagus (page 192).

1 cup sake or white wine

2 tablespoons minced peeled ginger root

1 cup chopped celery including some leaves

½ cup chopped scallion

½ teaspoon salt

½ teaspoon freshly ground black pepper

1½ pounds center-cut salmon fillet, skinned and
cut crosswise into 4 portions

3 tablespoons cold butter, cut into small pieces

In a large deep skillet, simmer the sake, ginger, celery, half the scallion, salt, and pepper for 30 minutes.

Put the salmon in the skillet, skinned side down. Cover and simmer the salmon for 10 minutes or until it is just cooked through. Carefully transfer it to a platter.

Boil the cooking liquid for 5 minutes, remove the pan from the heat, and swirl in the butter, stirring until the butter is incorporated. Serve the salmon with the sauce spooned on top.

Serves 4

simply poached salmon

Salmon is well suited to poaching—that is, gently simmering in water. This is a perfect way to prepare the fish for a salad or other chilled recipe, such as Salmon Cobb Salad with Creamy Mustard Dressing (page 102), Asian-Style Salmon Lettuce Rolls (page 104), or Poached Salmon with Cucumber-Yogurt Sauce (page 108).

6 cups water

2 tablespoons fresh lemon juice

1 small onion, chopped

2 celery ribs, including the leaves, chopped

3 fresh parsley sprigs

2 large thyme sprigs

1 teaspoon salt

1 bay leaf

freshly ground black pepper

2 pounds salmon fillet or steaks

In a large pot or deep skillet combine all the ingredients except the salmon. Simmer the mixture for 10 minutes to blend the flavors.

Add the salmon, skin side down, and poach it at a bare simmer for 8 to 10 minutes or until it is just cooked through. Transfer the salmon to a plate, cool, and chill.

NOTE: If you are short on time or ingredients, the salmon can simply be poached in the water with salt and pepper to taste. The salmon keeps for up to 2 days, covered and refrigerated.

Serves 4 to 6

salmon poached in lemon tomato broth

Over the last decades, as Americans became more health and fitness conscious, "spa" cuisine emerged. Chefs and resorts began offering highly seasoned, very lean options on their menus. Butter- and flour-thickened sauces were replaced with vegetable broths, and some of the techniques worked their way back into mainstream cuisine. One of the inspired ideas is poaching in tomato "water," or the thin liquid from fresh tomatoes. The flavors are clean and fresh, but pronounced and satisfying. If you need a little more filler with the dish, serve it over rice, noodles, orzo (rice-shaped pasta), or even mashed potatoes or Herbed Parmesan Grits (page 174).

1 28-ounce can whole peeled tomatoes (make sure they're not packed in tomato puree)

2 tablespoons fresh lemon juice

4 to 5 sprigs of fresh thyme or ½ teaspoon dried thyme

½ teaspoon salt

½ teaspoon sugar

¼ teaspoon freshly ground black pepper

1½ pounds skinned salmon fillet cut into 4 portions, or 4 salmon steaks (about 8 ounces each)

Set a fine sieve over a bowl. Empty the can of tomatoes into the sieve and squeeze the juice from 1 tomato at a time, letting the juice go through the sieve. Do not press the tomatoes through the sieve. Discard the solids or reserve them for another use. You want to extract 1½ to 2 cups of thin tomato juice.

In a deep skillet large enough to hold the salmon in one layer, combine the tomato liquid, lemon juice, thyme, salt, and pepper and bring to a boil. Add the salmon and poach it, at a bare simmer, for 10 minutes or until the salmon is just cooked through. Serve the salmon in shallow bowls with the broth.

Serves 4

salmon in grape sauce

One of my fondest childhood memories of special dinners is Sole Veronique, which my mother prepared beautifully. So I was not surprised, when I invited five friends over to taste four recipes, that the overall favorite was this dish. The juicy grapes, creamy sauce, and silken fish combine to create something luxurious and comforting. Seedless red or green grapes can be used, and the colors of both complement the pale pink of salmon beautifully. This dish can be dressed up for company with Sautéed Fennel and Apples (page 189), Watercress with Balsamic Vinegar and Butter (page 193), or rice and a salad for a quick dinner.

1 cup dry white wine

½ cup water

1 bay leaf

1 large shallot, minced, or ¼ cup minced onion

1½ pounds center-cut salmon fillet, skinned and
  cut crosswise into 4 portions

coarse kosher or sea salt

freshly ground black pepper

1 tablespoon butter

1 tablespoon all-purpose flour

¾ cup seedless red or green grapes, halved

2 tablespoons heavy cream

In a deep skillet with a lid, simmer together the wine, water, bay leaf, and shallot for 5 minutes. Season the salmon with salt and pepper and add to the skillet. Cover, and poach the salmon at a bare simmer for 8 to 10 minutes or until it is just cooked through.

Transfer the salmon to a plate and strain the cooking liquid through a sieve set over a bowl.

In the skillet, melt the butter over moderately low heat and add the flour. Cook this roux, stirring, for 2 minutes. Add the strained cooking liquid and the grapes. Simmer the sauce, whisking, for 2 minutes and whisk in the cream. Season the sauce with salt and pepper to taste and add the salmon just to reheat it.

Serves 4

salmon in mock tamarind sauce

Tamarind is a dark, sweet-and-sour fruit used in East Indian cuisine and many others around the world. Unfortunately it is not usually available at the average American grocery store, so I've substituted dried cranberries. This is not intended to be a universal substitute for tamarind, but the sweet/tart flavors are reminiscent of it. Basmati Rice, Currant, and Carrot Salad (page 180), and Peas and Rye Croutons (page 190) make colorful accompaniments.

½ cup sweetened dried cranberries (Craisins)

1 cup water

½ teaspoon turmeric

⅛ to ¼ teaspoon cayenne pepper

¼ cup fresh lemon juice

2 tablespoons vegetable oil

1½ pounds salmon fillet, skinned and cut into
   4 portions

coarse kosher or sea salt

freshly ground black pepper

2 teaspoons mustard seeds

Combine the cranberries and water in a small saucepan and simmer, covered, for 5 minutes. Puree the cranberries with the liquid in a blender or food processor and transfer to a sieve set over a bowl. Stir and force the puree through the sieve, discarding the solids. Stir the turmeric, cayenne, and lemon juice into the puree and set aside.

Heat the oil in a skillet over moderately high heat. Season the salmon with salt and pepper and sauté in the oil for 3 minutes on each side, or until browned. (It will not be cooked through.) Transfer the salmon to a plate.

Remove the skillet from the heat and add the mustard seeds to the hot oil remaining in the skillet. Cook the seeds, covered, about 15 seconds until the popping sound begins to dissipate. (The seeds will darken, but do not let them burn.) Immediately stir in the cranberry puree—be careful, as the mixture will spatter. Simmer the sauce, stirring, for 5 minutes, seasoning with salt and pepper and adding a little water if necessary to thin it to the consistency of a cream sauce.

Add the salmon and cook it in the sauce until it is just cooked through.

Serves 4

salmon cobb salad with creamy mustard dressing

This is a fresh way to use leftover salmon without it seeming like left-overs. Use any cooked salmon—grilled, baked, or poached.

THE DRESSING

½ cup mayonnaise

2½ tablespoons Dijon mustard

2 tablespoons fresh lemon juice

2 tablespoons water

2 teaspoons sugar

salt

freshly ground black pepper

1 pound cooked salmon, such as Simply Poached Salmon (page 95)

2 small ripe avocados

12 cups shredded romaine lettuce

4 hard-boiled eggs, chopped coarsely

12 cherry tomatoes, quartered

4 ounces soft mild goat cheese, crumbled

12 slices crisp cooked bacon, crumbled

In a bowl, whisk together the dressing ingredients until smooth. Season with salt and pepper.

Discard any skin and bones from the salmon and break it into large pieces.

Peel and pit the avocados and chop them coarsely.

Divide the lettuce among four plates or large bowls and divide the remaining ingredients among the salads, topping them with the salmon and bacon.

Drizzle the dressing over the salads or serve it on the side.

Serves 4

asian-style salmon lettuce rolls

These are a cross between California rolls (a popular kind of sushi) and Vietnamese finger foods that are wrapped in lettuce. Serve them as an appetizer or a light luncheon entrée, with Gingered Spaghetti Squash (page 196) and Fried Corn and Peppers with Butter and Basil (page 191).

2 tablespoons rice vinegar

1 teaspoon toasted sesame seed oil

¼ cup vegetable oil

½ cup chopped scallion

salt

freshly ground black pepper

1 pound Simply Poached Salmon (page 95)

2 ripe avocados, peeled, pitted, and sliced

2 cups cooked rice (preferably short-grain, i.e. sushi rice), cooled

8 whole lettuce leaves (such as Boston, Bibb, or iceberg),
   rinsed and patted dry

hot chili sauce (optional)

Whisk together the vinegar, oils, and scallion until the dressing is emulsified, and season with salt and pepper.

The remaining ingredients can be put on separate plates and diners can assemble their own rolls, or they can be assembled and served on a platter. Down the middle of a lettuce leaf arrange some rice, avocado slices, and salmon. Spoon some dressing on top. Season with chili sauce if desired. Roll the filling up in the lettuce and eat out of hand.

Makes 8 large rolls serving 8 as an appetizer or 4 as a luncheon entrée

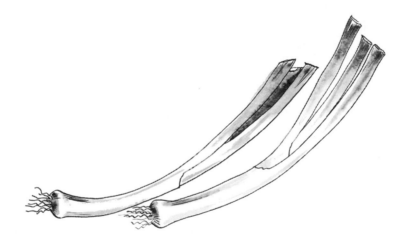

seared salmon with mesclun and raspberry vermouth vinaigrette

This quick, light main-course salad is just the thing for a warm summer night and elegant enough for a formal luncheon. It is also a great way to use leftover salmon.

¼ cup raspberry vinegar

¼ cup plus 3 tablespoons vegetable or olive oil

1 tablespoon honey

1 tablespoon dry vermouth (optional)

salt

freshly ground black pepper

1½ pounds skinned salmon fillet, cut into 4 portions

8 cups mesclun (mixed baby greens), rinsed and spun dry

Whisk together the vinegar, ¼ cup plus 2 tablespoons of oil, honey, vermouth, salt, and pepper until emulsified.

Put the salmon on a plate and rub with the remaining tablespoon of oil. Season it with salt and pepper.

Heat a nonstick skillet over moderate heat and add the salmon. Cook for about 5 minutes on each side and transfer to a plate.

In a large bowl, toss the lettuce with half the dressing. Divide salad among four plates and top with salmon. Drizzle remaining dressing over the salmon.

NOTE: To prepare in advance, have the lettuce washed, spun dry, and chilled; the dressing made; and the salmon cooked and at room temperature. Assemble the dish when ready to serve.

Serves 4

poached salmon with cucumber-yogurt sauce

This salmon is delicious served hot, warm, room temperature, or chilled. Whether served in the dead of winter or the hottest day of summer, this versatile winner is sure to please. Serve with Blasted Vegetables (page 188), Egg Noodles with Tomato (page 177) or Basmati Rice, Currant, and Carrot Salad (page 180).

FOR SAUCE

1 cup plain yogurt

2 cups peeled, seeded, and chopped cucumber

¼ cup minced fresh dill

1 small garlic clove, minced

2 tablespoons minced scallion

1 tablespoon olive oil

¼ teaspoon salt

¼ teaspoon freshly ground black pepper or
   ⅛ teaspoon cayenne pepper

1½ pounds Simply Poached Salmon (page 95)

Stir together all ingredients for the sauce and let stand at room temperature for thirty minutes.

Arrange the salmon on a platter and top with the sauce.

NOTE: Whole-milk yogurt can be hard to find in the grocery store, but tastes the best here. Low-fat yogurt is okay to use, but nonfat yogurt produces a chalky, insipid sauce, hardly worth the savings in calories.

The sauce can be made 1 day in advance and kept covered and refrigerated. Allow it to come to room temperature before serving.

Serves 4

salmon and yellow pepper chowder

The beautiful colors of yellow, pink, and green make this chowder as good to look at as it is to eat. Red bell peppers can certainly be substituted for the yellow, but green peppers do not have the same sweetness. A salad and some good bread are all you need to add for a satisfying summer supper. Any leftovers freeze well.

3 medium leeks, trimmed, washed well and
   sliced thin (see Note)

3 yellow bell peppers, diced

2 garlic cloves, minced

2 celery ribs, chopped

1 bay leaf

2 tablespoons butter

4 small red potatoes (¾ to 1 pound)

2 8-ounce bottles clam juice

1½ cups water

1 cup heavy cream

salt

freshly ground black pepper

1 pound salmon fillet, skinned

2 tablespoons minced fresh dill

In a large pot, cook the leeks, peppers, garlic, celery, and bay leaf in the butter over moderate heat, stirring, for 15 minutes. Add the potatoes, clam juice, and water and simmer for 15 minutes. Discard the bay leaf. Remove 1 cup of the soup mixture and puree it in a blender or food processor. Stir the puree and cream into the soup. Season the soup with salt and pepper.

Feel the salmon with the fingertips to make sure there are no bones remaining and cut it into 1-inch cubes. Bring the soup to a simmer and add the salmon. Simmer it gently for 10 to 12 minutes or until the salmon is cooked through. Stir in the dill.

NOTE: Leeks add a distinctive delicate flavor, but their grit can ruin a dish. Always wash them carefully. Trim the root ends and the tough dark green leaves from the leeks. Split each leek lengthwise to within ½-inch of the root end. With the leafy end hanging down, wash each leek under running water, separating each leaf to get out all the dirt.

The soup can be made ahead and frozen for up to 1 month or refrigerated for 1 day. Add the dill after gently reheating.

Makes 10 cups

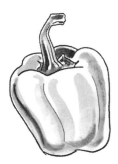

fish steaks

Chili-Rubbed Halibut with Mexican Pickled Onions

Potato-Crusted Halibut with Chive Sour Cream Sauce

Roasted Halibut with Onion Wine Sauce

Baked Halibut Georgiana

Halibut Steak Baked with Roasted Jalapeño Tartar Sauce

Halibut Stewed with Tomatoes and White Beans

Halibut in Lemon Sauce

Nut-Crusted Halibut

Halibut in Basil Corn Broth

Halibut with Beets

Swordfish with Onions, Raisins, and Pine Nuts

Swordfish Poached in Curried Tomato Sauce

Roasted Swordfish Cuban-Style

Grilled Swordfish in Flank Steak Marinade

Curried Swordfish Kebabs with Pineapple and Carrot Salsa

Marmalade-Marinated Swordfish

Swordfish in Curried Pumpkin Sauce with Sunflower and Pomegranate Seeds

Swordfish and Mushroom Marsala

Swordfish Schnitzel

Grilled Swordfish Dijon

Grilled Sangria Swordfish

Grilled Lemon-Pepper Tuna Kebabs with Chive Mayonnaise

Grilled Tuna with Tahini Parsley Sauce

Tuna Grilled Korean-Style

Seared Tuna with Port and Figs

Grilled Tuna Marinated in Carrot and Basil Sauce

Grilled Tuna and Peppers Sandwich with Herb Mayonnaise

Tuna Roasted on Leeks, Potatoes, and Sage

Tuna in Garlic Caramel Sauce

Fresh Tuna Salad

NOTE FOR ALL TUNA RECIPES

If you refuse to eat any rare fish, then do not cook tuna steak. Fresh tuna should never be cooked well done because it turns dry and chalky. I find the compromise between raw and well done is to leave a band of red through the middle when removed from the pan or grill (3 to 4 minutes per side). It will continue to cook slightly from the residual heat.

If any hint of pink is still too rare for you, then substitute swordfish, which should never be served rare.

chili-rubbed halibut with mexican pickled onions

A variation of this Mexican onion condiment is referred to as the ketchup of the Yucatán Peninsula, a reflection of its popularity. The spicy, sweet-and-sour flavor and crisp texture is indeed addictive and complements many dishes, including this grilled chili halibut. To round out the meal, serve with Quick Rice and Beans (page 178) and Fried Corn and Peppers with Butter and Basil (page 191).

2 tablespoons fresh lime juice

2 teaspoons chili powder

2 tablespoons vegetable oil

2 tablespoons grated onion

¾ teaspoon coarse kosher or sea salt

4 halibut steaks (about 8 ounces each)

Mexican Pickled Onions (recipe follows)

In a bowl, whisk together all the ingredients except the halibut and onions. Put the halibut in a plastic bag and add the marinade, making sure the fish is coated thoroughly. Seal the bag and marinate in the refrigerator for 30 minutes to 1 hour.

Preheat a grill, or broiler with rack in the top position.

Brush the grill with vegetable oil and grill halibut (or broil it on a rack set in a baking pan) 6 minutes on each side or until just cooked through. Serve with the Mexican pickled onions.

NOTE: Swordfish, tuna, or any other fish steak can be substituted for the halibut.

Serves 4

mexican pickled onions

1 pound red onions (2 medium), sliced thin into rings

1 small fresh jalapeño chili, sliced into very thin rings
(see Note), seeded if less "heat" is desired

¾ cup distilled white vinegar

¼ cup water

½ cup fresh orange juice

1 teaspoon cumin seeds

1 teaspoon dried oregano

1½ teaspoons salt

1 tablespoon sugar

In a large saucepan, combine onions and enough water to cover. Bring water to a boil and drain. Return the onions to the saucepan and add the remaining ingredients. Bring mixture to a boil and transfer to a heatproof glass or ceramic bowl. Cool and refrigerate, covered, for 24 hours.

NOTE: Wear rubber gloves when handling, seeding, and chopping chilis. The oils that make the chili hot are not easily rinsed from the hands and can be very irritating when touched to the eyes or mouth.

Covered and refrigerated, the onions will keep for one month.

Makes about 2 cups

potato-crusted halibut with chive sour cream sauce

When tired of thinking creatively in his own field, my husband enjoys coming up with ideas for new recipes. Some of them I quickly dismiss, like his idea for preparing fish encased in a potato pancake.

"Too complicated for the home cook," I replied. "These recipes are supposed to be simple!"

"Well, then, what if you used instant potato flakes?"

"Potato flakes? I couldn't possibly lower my standards to even buy a box of potato flakes. How could I call for it in a recipe?"

"Why not? Isn't it just dehydrated potatoes?"

Why not indeed? What makes fried potatoes crisp is the starch content, once the water has evaporated. Instant potatoes have taken a step out of the process. They produce a crisp, light coating, and they work beautifully on shrimp, too.

4 halibut steaks (about 8 ounces each)

coarse kosher or sea salt

freshly ground black pepper

1 large egg

¾ cup instant potato flakes

vegetable oil for frying

Chive Sour Cream Sauce (recipe follows)
  or lemon wedges

Trim the skin from the steaks and season with salt and pepper.

Put the egg in a shallow dish and beat it lightly to blend. Dip the steaks in the egg, coating each well. Then dredge them in the potato flakes, patting and pressing them onto the fish. Cover and refrigerate the steaks for at least 1 hour and up to 8 hours.

In a large deep skillet, heat ¼ inch of vegetable oil over moderately high heat until very hot but not smoking. Add the coated steaks and fry for about 5 minutes on each side or until crisp and browned. Drain them briefly on brown paper, and serve immediately with the sauce or lemon wedges.

NOTE: Letting the fish stand in the refrigerator after coating allows the potato flakes to adhere better.

Serves 4

chive sour cream sauce

½ cup sour cream
2 tablespoons mayonnaise
3 tablespoons minced fresh chives
1 tablespoon lemon juice
½ teaspoon minced garlic
salt
freshly ground black pepper

Stir together all ingredients. Refrigerate until ready to serve. Covered and refrigerated, the sauce will keep up to 2 days.

roasted halibut with onion wine sauce

The wine red of the onions against the stark white of the fish makes this dish as satisfying to look at as it is to devour. Serve it with Mashed White Beans and Garlic (page 182), Old Bay Seasoned Roasted New Potatoes (page 171), or Herbed Parmesan Grits (page 174).

FOR SAUCE

2 cups sliced onion (about one large onion)

1 garlic clove, minced

2 teaspoons olive oil

⅓ cup dry red wine

¼ cup water

2 teaspoons sugar

coarse kosher or sea salt

freshly ground black pepper

4 halibut steaks (about 8 ounces each)

In a nonstick skillet, cook the onion and garlic in oil, stirring over moderately low heat until onions are pale golden and translucent. Add the wine, water, sugar, salt, and pepper and simmer the sauce for 2 minutes.

Preheat the oven to 450°F.

Season the halibut with salt and pepper and arrange it in a single layer in a baking dish. Top with the onion sauce. Roast in the oven for 15 to 20 minutes or until the fish is just cooked through.

NOTE: The sauce can be made 1 day in advance, kept covered and refrigerated.

Serves 4

baked halibut georgiana

My friend Georgiana developed this recipe using a distinctive flavor combination from her homeland, Sierra Leone: cilantro, nutmeg, allspice, and ginger. Balsamic vinegar is her favorite "new" ingredient, which she incorporates into much of her cooking. Couscous with Dried Cranberries and Buttered Almonds (page 175) or Herbed Parmesan Grits (page 174) are two of many possible side dishes. This dish is easily doubled or tripled for a crowd.

1 large onion, sliced thin

1 green bell pepper, sliced thin

¼ cup chopped fresh cilantro

2 tablespoons balsamic vinegar

2 tablespoons dry sherry

⅛ teaspoon nutmeg

⅛ teaspoon ground allspice

1 teaspoon minced peeled fresh ginger

4 halibut steaks (about 8 ounces each)

coarse kosher or sea salt

freshly ground black pepper

Combine all ingredients up to the fish in a bowl and toss well. Spread half the mixture in the bottom of a large baking dish. Season the halibut on both sides with salt and pepper and put on top of the vegetables. Scatter the remaining mixture on top.

Preheat oven to 425°F.

Bake the fish 13 to 15 minutes or until cooked through. Serve the halibut with the vegetables and juices spooned on top.

NOTE: The dish can be assembled ahead of time and kept covered and refrigerated for up to 4 hours before baking.

Serves 4

halibut steak baked with roasted jalapeño tartar sauce

The spiciness of this sauce combined with the richness of the mayonnaise produces a luscious moist fish with a sophisticated twist. Serve with Peas and Rye Croutons (page 190), Zesty Asparagus (page 192), and Egg Noodles with Tomato (page 177). The tartar sauce is also great to have on hand to accompany leftover fish or to spread on a sandwich.

1 or 2 fresh jalapeño chilis
½ cup mayonnaise (regular or reduced-fat)
2 tablespoons finely chopped sour pickle
2 tablespoons chopped fresh parsley or basil
3 tablespoons minced scallion
1 tablespoon fresh lemon juice
salt
4 halibut steaks (about 8 ounces each)

Preheat oven to 400°F.

Roast the jalapeños by setting a wire rack on a stove, over a gas flame or hot electric burner. Put the chilis on the rack and turn them with tongs until browned on all sides. Wrap chilis in a paper towel until cooled.

Wearing rubber gloves, cut the jalapeño flesh away from the stem and seeds, and chop it fine (see Note).

In a small bowl, stir together the mayonnaise, pickle, parsley, scallion, and lemon juice. Add the chopped jalapeño to taste and season with salt.

Arrange the halibut in a single layer in a baking dish and spread about ¼ cup of the sauce on top of each steak. Reserve any remaining sauce to serve on the side.

Bake for 18 to 20 minutes or until fish is cooked through.

NOTE: Do not peel away the browned skin from the jalapeños as you would for roasted bell peppers. The skin is tender and adds a nice smoky flavor to the sauce.

Bottled pepperoncini peppers can be substituted for the roasted jalapeños. If a mild sauce is preferred, use bottled roasted red bell peppers in place of the roasted jalapeños.

The sauce can be made up to 2 days in advance, kept covered and refrigerated.

Swordfish can be substituted.

Serves 4

halibut stewed with tomatoes and white beans

The flavors of Tuscany inspired this soothing one-dish meal. As it is a cross between a soupy stew and a pasta sauce, a country-style Italian bread is helpful to get every drop of the juices.

3 garlic cloves, minced

1 medium onion, coarsely chopped

1 tablespoon olive oil

1 28-ounce can whole plum tomatoes, drained

½ teaspoon dried thyme

¼ teaspoon fennel seed

½ teaspoon sugar

1 bay leaf

1 15½ ounce can small white beans, drained and rinsed

4 halibut steaks, about 8 ounces each

coarse kosher or sea salt

freshly ground black pepper

¾ pound dried pasta such as fusilli, rotini, or egg noodles

¼ cup minced fresh parsley

freshly grated Parmesan cheese as an accompaniment

In a large skillet, cook the garlic and onion in oil over low heat, stirring, until softened. Add the tomatoes—breaking them up—and the thyme, fennel, sugar, and bay leaf. Simmer, stirring occasionally, for 30 minutes.

Stir the beans into the skillet. Season the halibut with salt and pepper and put on top of the bean mixutre. Simmer, covered, 10 to 12 minutes, or until fish is cooked through.

Meanwhile boil the pasta in a kettle of rapidly boiling salted water until al dente, and drain.

Divide the pasta among four shallow bowls and spoon the fish and sauce on top. Sprinkle each serving with the parsley and serve the Parmesan separately.

NOTE: Tuna or swordfish can be substituted.

Serves 4

halibut in lemon sauce

Toasted Vermicelli and Herbs (page 176), and Braised Escarole with Tomatoes and Garlic (page 184) make delicious accompaniments to this lemony, buttery fish.

4 halibut steaks (about 8 ounces each)

coarse kosher or sea salt

freshly ground black pepper

½ cup plus 1 tablespoon all-purpose flour

2 tablespoons vegetable oil

4 tablespoons butter

3 tablespoons fresh lemon juice

¾ cup chicken broth

½ cup water

2 tablespoons minced fresh parsley

Season the steaks with salt and pepper and dredge them in ½ cup of the flour, coating them thoroughly.

Heat the oil over moderately high heat until it is hot. Add the halibut and cook it for 5 minutes on each side or until just cooked through. Reduce the heat to moderate if the fish begins to burn.

Transfer the halibut to a plate and wipe the skillet clean. In the skillet, cook the remaining 1 tablespoon of flour in the butter over low heat, stirring, for 2 minutes. Add the lemon juice, chicken broth, and water, and boil the sauce, whisking, until thickened. Season with salt and pepper and serve on top of the halibut. Garnish each serving with the parsley.

Serves 4

nut-crusted halibut

The nut crust locks in the juices of the delicate white-fleshed fish while adding a deep, rich flavor. Contrasting acidic, sweet, and bitter flavors go well with this dish to cut the richness. Collard Greens with a Northern Accent (page 204), Grilled Ratatouille Salad (page 186), Broiled Ripe Plantains (page 194), and Sauteed Fennel and Apples (page 189) all make fine accompaniments.

4 halibut steaks (about 8 ounces each)

coarse kosher or sea salt

freshly ground black pepper

¼ cup all-purpose flour

2 large eggs, lightly beaten

1 cup finely chopped peanuts, pecans, or cashews

1 tablespoon butter

2 tablespoons vegetable oil

Lemon or lime wedges as an accompaniment

Season the steaks with salt and pepper. Dredge them in the flour, coating them thoroughly. Dip each in the egg, then coat with the nuts.

In a large skillet, heat the butter and the oil over moderate heat until hot. Add the halibut and sauté for 5 to 7 minutes on each side, or until the outside is crisp and the fish is just cooked through. Serve with the lemon wedges.

Serves 4

halibut in basil corn broth

Boil some extra corn one night, save the water, and serve this healthy, tasty dish the next night. Serve it over noodles or rice, or in soup bowls with crusty bread on the side.

2 cooked ears of corn on the cob
2 cups corn water reserved from boiling corn
1 tomato, diced
⅓ cup chopped scallion
2 pounds halibut steak, cut into 8 pieces
salt
freshly ground black pepper
¼ cup finely chopped fresh basil
¼ cup chopped fresh cilantro
1 to 2 tablespoons fresh lime juice

Cut the corn from the cob and scrape the cobs with the back of a knife to extract all the juices and pulp.

In a large deep skillet or pot, combine the corn, corn water, tomato, and scallion and bring to a boil. Season the halibut with salt and pepper and add to the pan. Simmer, uncovered, shaking the pot occasionally, for 10 minutes or until the fish is just cooked through.

Stir in the herbs and lime juice to taste.

NOTE: For an impressive presentation, you can serve this dish in the style of a Vietnamese noodle shop. Ladle it into large bowls and pass a tray consisting of thinly sliced fresh jalapeños, plenty of whole mint, cilantro, and basil leaves, bean sprouts, and lime wedges. Diners may top their bowls with the condiments they desire.

Serves 4

halibut with beets

Classic borscht ingredients—beets, dill, and horseradish—team up with halibut to provide a fresh and tasty entrée. To make a meal, serve with Cauliflower with Caramelized Onions and Poppy Seeds (page 185), or Old Bay Seasoned Roasted New Potatoes (page 171).

3 tablespoons olive oil

4 halibut steaks (about 8 ounces each)

coarse kosher or sea salt

freshly ground black pepper

2 pounds fresh beets, trimmed, scrubbed, and thinly sliced (reserve beet greens to make greens with balsamic vinegar (see page 193) if desired)

½ cup water

1 teaspoon bottled horseradish

¼ cup minced fresh dill

In a large nonstick skillet, heat the oil over moderately high heat until it is hot but not smoking. Season the halibut with salt and pepper and sauté the steaks for 6 minutes on each side or until golden brown and just cooked through. Transfer the fish to a plate and keep it warm, covered loosely.

Add the beets and water to the skillet and simmer, covered, for 10 minutes, or until the beets are tender. Stir in the horseradish, salt, and pepper.

Divide the beet mixture among four plates and top with the halibut. Sprinkle each serving with some of the dill.

NOTE: This dish is a beautiful, shocking contrast of colors. Wear rubber gloves if you want to protect your hands from staining while slicing the beets.

Serves 4

swordfish with onions, raisins, and pine nuts

This sublime combination of fruit and nuts with sweet spices was inspired by the complex cuisines of the eastern Mediterranean. Suitable accompaniments would be plain couscous or rice to absorb the juices, warm pita bread, and a salad.

⅓ cup pine nuts

2 tablespoons olive oil

2 small onions, quartered lengthwise

1 bay leaf

⅔ cup raisins

½ teaspoon cinnamon

2 tablespoons fresh lemon juice

1 cup water

salt

freshly ground black pepper

2 pounds swordfish, cut into 4 portions

⅓ cup coarsely chopped parsley leaves

In a deep skillet, cook the pine nuts in olive oil over moderate heat, stirring, for about 3 minutes or until golden. Remove nuts with a slotted spoon and reserve.

Add the onions to the skillet and cook, stirring, for about five minutes or until they begin to brown. Add the bay leaf, raisins, cinnamon, lemon juice, and water and simmer, stirring, for 5 minutes. Season with salt and pepper.

Add the fish and poach at a bare simmer, covered, for 10 minutes or until just cooked through. Divide the fish among four plates, top with sauce, and sprinkle with parsley and the reserved pine nuts.

NOTE: The sauce can be made 1 day in advance, kept covered and refrigerated. Reheat before adding the fish.

Halibut can be substituted.

Serves 4

swordfish poached in curried tomato sauce

Some fish markets sell swordfish cubes for kebabs, which they cut from pieces of swordfish too small to sell as steaks. They can be significantly cheaper, but make sure they are not giving you the dark muscle and ask if the chunks are as fresh as the steaks. Couscous with Dried Cranberries and Buttered Almonds (page 175) makes a perfect accompaniment.

FOR SAUCE

    1 cup chopped onion (about 1 small onion)

    1 tablespoon vegetable oil

    2 large tomatoes, chopped (about 2½ cups)

    2 teaspoons curry powder

    ½ teaspoon salt

    ¼ teaspoon sugar

    2 tablespoons chopped fresh cilantro or parsley

    1½ pounds swordfish, trimmed of skin, dark meat, and fat, and cut into 2-inch chunks

    salt

    freshly ground black pepper

In a large deep skillet, cook the onion in oil over moderate heat, stirring, until it begins to color. Add the tomatoes, curry, salt, and sugar and simmer, uncovered, for 15 minutes, stirring occasionally.

Add the swordfish and simmer, stirring occasionally, for 10 minutes or until it is cooked through. Season with salt and pepper.

Divide the fish among four plates, spoon the sauce on top, and sprinkle with cilantro.

NOTE: Any fish steak can be substituted.

Serves 4

roasted swordfish cuban-style

This combination of seasonings is based on the delectable Cuban marinade for pork and chicken. Serve it with Blasted Sweet Potatoes with Salt, Malt Vinegar, and Parsley (page 170) or Quick Rice and Beans (page 178).

2 tablespoons fresh lemon juice

½ teaspoon salt

¼ teaspoon freshly ground black pepper

½ teaspoon dried oregano

½ teaspoon ground cumin

2 garlic cloves, minced

1 tablespoon olive oil

1 small onion, sliced thin

4 6-ounce swordfish steaks (¾ to 1 inch thick)

Preheat oven to 425°F.

Combine all the ingredients except the fish. Arrange the swordfish in a baking dish large enough to hold it in a single layer. Rub the steaks with the spice mixture and immediately bake for 13 to 15 minutes or until cooked through. Serve immediately.

NOTE: Tuna or halibut can be substituted, but tuna should be cooked for a shorter time.

Serves 4

grilled swordfish in flank steak marinade

The appealing combination of soy sauce, lemon, and garlic, my standard marinade for flank steak, also complements swordfish beautifully. Try serving it with Mashed White Beans and Garlic (page 182) or Skinny Scalloped Potatoes (page 172) and Braised Escarole with Tomatoes and Garlic (page 184).

3 tablespoons soy sauce

2 tablespoons fresh lemon juice

2 tablespoons vegetable oil, plus additional for brushing the grill

1 garlic clove, minced or forced through a garlic press

½ teaspoon sugar

¼ teaspoon salt

½ teaspoon freshly ground black pepper

4 6-ounce swordfish steaks (¾ to 1 inch thick)

In a large plastic bag or large shallow dish, blend together all ingredients except the swordfish. Add the swordfish, coating it well with marinade, and let it marinate, covered and refrigerated, 30 minutes to 2 hours.

Preheat a grill, or broiler with rack in the top position.

Brush the grill with vegetable oil. Discard the marinade and grill the fish (or broil it on a rack set in a baking pan), for 5 minutes on each side or until just cooked through. Serve immediately.

NOTE: Tuna, shark, or halibut can be substituted, but tuna should be cooked for a shorter time.

Serves 4

curried swordfish kebabs with pineapple and carrot salsa

Plain rice or Couscous with Dried Cranberries and Buttered Almonds (page 175) makes a marvelous dinner partner.

2 tablespoons vegetable oil

1 tablespoon curry powder

1 tablespoon soy sauce

2 teaspoons honey

salt

freshly ground black pepper

1½ pounds swordfish, trimmed of skin, dark meat, and fat, and cut into 1½-inch chunks

Pineapple and Carrot Salsa (recipe follows)

In a bowl, whisk together the oil, curry powder, soy, honey, salt, and pepper. Add the fish to the marinade and toss until coated well. Cover and refrigerate at least 30 minutes and up to 3 hours.

Preheat a grill, or broiler with rack in the top position.

Thread the fish cubes, corner to corner, onto skewers.

Brush the grill with vegetable oil and grill the kebabs (or broil them on a rack set in a baking pan) for about 5 minutes on each side or until just cooked through. Serve with the salsa.

NOTE: Bamboo skewers can be used. Before using, immerse them in water for at least 30 minutes to prevent them from burning during cooking.

Threading the fish cubes corner to corner allows the fish to cook through evenly without being raw where the cubes touch.

Serves 4

pineapple and carrot salsa

⅔ cup chopped fresh or canned pineapple
   (reserve 2 tablespoons juice)

⅔ cup shredded carrot (1 large carrot)

2 tablespoons fresh lime juice

3 tablespoons minced fresh chives or scallion greens

1 fresh hot chili pepper, minced, or ¼ teaspoon dried
   hot red pepper flakes (optional)

½ teaspoon salt

2 tablespoons chopped fresh basil leaves

In a small bowl, stir together salsa ingredients. Refrigerate, covered, for at least 30 minutes and up to 24 hours.

Makes about 1½ cups

marmalade-marinated swordfish

The marmalade caramelizes on the fish during the grilling, adding a subtle, dark sweetness to this quick and tasty fish. Serve it with Watercress with Balsamic Vinegar and Butter (page 193) and Fried Rice with Ham and Pineapple (page 179).

½ cup orange marmalade

2 tablespoons soy sauce

1 tablespoon wine vinegar

1 teaspoon ground coriander seed

½ teaspoon hot red pepper flakes

1½ pounds swordfish (about 1 inch thick)
   cut into 4 portions

coarse kosher or sea salt

vegetable oil for brushing the grill

In a large plastic bag, blend together all the ingredients except the fish, salt, and oil. Add the fish, making sure each piece is coated with the marinade, and seal the bag. Let the fish marinate in the refrigerator for at least 1 hour and up to 4 hours.

Remove the fish from the bag. Transfer the marinade to a saucepan, and simmer it gently, stirring, for 5 minutes. Strain through a fine sieve set over a bowl. Discard the solids and return the sauce to the pan.

Preheat a grill, or broiler with rack in the top position.

Season the swordfish with salt. Brush the grill with oil and grill the swordfish (or broil it on a rack set in a baking pan) for 5 to 6 minutes on each side or until just cooked through. Reheat the sauce and serve on the side with the fish.

NOTE: Tuna or halibut can be substituted, but tuna should be cooked for a shorter time.

Serves 4

swordfish in curried pumpkin sauce with sunflower and pomegranate seeds

The vibrant colors and flavors of this dish dazzle the eyes and please the palate. Add bright green Peas and Rye Croutons (page 190) to the plate and you've created a masterpiece.

1 cup chopped onion

2 tablespoons olive oil

1 tablespoon plus 1 teaspoon curry powder

1½ cups canned chicken broth

½ cup canned pumpkin puree (make sure you don't use pumpkin pie filling)

1 tablespoon fresh lime juice

salt

freshly ground black pepper

1½ pounds swordfish steak, cut into 4 portions

roasted sunflower seeds and pomegranate seeds (see Note) for garnish

In a large deep skillet, cook the onion in the oil over moderate heat, stirring until softened. Add the curry powder and cook, stirring, for 2 minutes. Stir in the broth, pumpkin, lime juice, salt, and pepper. Simmer for 2 minutes.

Add the swordfish and cook, covered, at a bare simmer, for 5 minutes. Turn the fish over and continue to simmer, covered, 5 minutes more or until it is just cooked through.

Divide the fish among four plates and spoon the sauce on top. Sprinkle with the seeds.

NOTE: Pomegranates, those leathery-looking red fruits with a spout that appear in markets in the fall, contain dazzling-looking and -tasting juicy sweet/tart seeds. Cut the fruit open and free the ruby seeds from the bitter white membrane within. They are a treat eaten straight, or sprinkled on salads and dishes like the one above.

Halibut can be substituted.

Serves 4

swordfish and mushroom marsala

Swordfish replaces the veal cutlet in this Italian favorite. This dish is elegant and comforting at the same time. Add a salad and rice or Skinny Scalloped Potatoes (page 172).

2 pounds swordfish steak (about 1 inch thick),
   cut into 4 portions

coarse kosher or sea salt

freshly ground black pepper

¼ cup all-purpose flour

2 tablespoons butter

1 tablespoon olive oil

1½ pounds mushrooms, wiped clean and sliced

¾ cup dry Marsala

⅓ cup chopped fresh parsley

Season the swordfish steaks on both sides with salt and pepper and dredge them in the flour.

In a skillet large enough to hold the steaks without crowding, heat the butter and oil over moderately high heat until very hot. Add the steaks and brown for 4 to 5 minutes on each side. They will not be completely cooked through. Transfer the fish to a plate.

Reduce the heat to moderate. In the skillet, cook the mushrooms, stirring, for 8 to 10 minutes or until softened. Add the Marsala, salt, and pepper, and simmer, stirring, for 5 minutes. Stir in the parsley and return the steaks to the skillet. Simmer, covered, until the steaks are reheated, about 3 minutes.

NOTE: Halibut can be substituted.

Serves 4

swordfish schnitzel

Just like the classic veal version, this schnitzel is juicy and tender on the inside with an irresistible crispy crust. The traditional Austrian accompaniments can be found with a twist in Cucumber and Onion Salad with Yogurt Cumin Vinaigrette (page 202) and Old Bay Seasoned Roasted New Potatoes (page 171).

2 1-pound swordfish steaks, at least 1 inch thick, trimmed of skin

coarse kosher or sea salt

freshly ground black pepper

about ½ cup all-purpose flour

2 large eggs, beaten lightly

1 cup fresh bread crumbs

vegetable oil for frying

lemon wedges

Lay a swordfish steak on a work surface. Using a long, sharp knife, carefully halve each steak horizontally, to yield 4 steaks about ½ inch thick. Season them with salt and pepper.

Have the flour, eggs, and bread crumbs ready in separate shallow bowls. Dredge each steak in the flour, shaking off the excess. Dip it in the egg, coating it thoroughly, and dredge it in the bread crumbs.

In two very large skillets, heat ¼ inch oil over moderately high heat until it is hot but not smoking, and in it fry the steaks for 4 minutes on each side or until deep brown and crisp. Serve immediately, with lemon wedges.

Serves 4

grilled swordfish dijon

The mayonnaise in the sauce forms a slight crust on the fish while keeping it very moist. This makes a simply glorious summer meal with fresh tomatoes and basil and corn on the cob.

½ cup mayonnaise (reduced-fat may be used)

3 tablespoons Dijon mustard

2 teaspoons fresh lemon juice

1½ pounds swordfish steak, trimmed of any dark meat and divided into 4 portions

coarse kosher or sea salt

freshly ground black pepper

In a small bowl, stir together all the ingredients up to the fish. Reserve 3 tablespoons of the sauce and keep it covered and refrigerated.

Season the fish steaks with salt and pepper and spread them with the remaining sauce, coating all sides.

Preheat a grill, or broiler with rack in the top position.

Brush the grill with oil and grill the swordfish (or broil it on a rack set in a baking pan) for 6 minutes on one side. Turn the steaks and spread the reserved sauce on top. Grill 6 minutes more or until just cooked through.

NOTE: The fish can be coated with the sauce in advance and refrigerated for up to 8 hours.

Any other fish steak can be substituted.

Serves 4

grilled sangria swordfish

The fish can be served plain, without the sangria sauce, if desired. Serve it with Fried Corn and Peppers with Butter and Basil (page 191), Sautéed Fennel and Apples (page 189), or Cucumber and Onion Salad with Yogurt Cumin Vinaigrette (page 202).

3 cups light-bodied red wine, such as
   merlot or Beaujolais

⅓ cup sugar

1 lemon, sliced thin and ends discarded

1 orange, sliced thin and ends discarded

4 whole cloves

1 tablespoon vanilla

¼ cup vegetable oil

1½ pounds swordfish steak (about 1 inch thick),
   cut into 4 portions

coarse kosher or sea salt

freshly ground black pepper

4 tablespoons butter, softened and cut into pieces

In a stainless saucepan, boil the wine, sugar, fruit, and cloves until the wine is reduced to 1 cup. Strain the mixture over a bowl, pressing on the fruit to extract the juice. Discard the solids. Stir in the vanilla and chill the sangria.

Reserve ¼ cup of the sangria in a small saucepan for the sauce. Whisk the oil into the remaining sangria and add it to a large plastic bag or dish with the swordfish. Marinate the fish, covered and refrigerated, for at least 2 hours and up to 6 hours.

Preheat a grill, or broiler with rack in the top position.

Remove the swordfish from the bag and discard the marinade. Season the swordfish with salt and pepper.

Brush the grill with oil and grill the swordfish (or broil it on a rack set in a baking pan) for 6 minutes on each side or until just cooked through.

Bring the reserved sangria to a boil, remove the pan from the heat, and whisk in the butter until it is incorporated. Season with salt and pepper. Nap the steaks with the sauce.

NOTE: Tuna, shark, or halibut can be substituted.

Serves 4

grilled lemon-pepper tuna kebabs with chive mayonnaise

Bottled lemon pepper is made with dehydrated lemon zest, which lacks the intense flavor of the oils in fresh zest. The method used here for removing the zest can be used for any recipe calling for zest. It is a good way to ensure that you don't include the bitter white pith, while getting the most of the yellow zest and oils. Serve these kebabs with Grilled Ratatouille Salad (page 186) and Green Salad with Grapes and Walnuts (page 205).

3 lemons

1½ teaspoons kosher or sea salt

¾ teaspoon freshly ground black pepper

½ teaspoon sugar

1½ pounds tuna steak, cut into 2-inch cubes

FOR THE MAYONNAISE

½ cup mayonnaise (reduced-fat can be used)

3 tablespoons fresh lemon juice

¼ cup minced fresh chives

¾ teaspoon Worcestershire sauce

salt

freshly ground black pepper

Rinse the lemons in warm water and dry them. Remove the thin yellow zest from the lemons with a vegetable peeler. If there is any white pith on the interior side of the zest strips, remove it with the peeler or a sharp knife. Mince the zest very fine and transfer to a small bowl. Add the salt, pepper, and sugar. Blend the mixture until it resembles wet sand.

Thread the tuna cubes onto metal skewers corner to corner, so they cook in between. Sprinkle the lemon mixture on top. Cover and refrigerate for up to four hours.

In a small bowl, whisk together the mayonnaise, lemon juice, chives, Worcestershire, salt, and pepper.

Preheat a grill, or broiler with rack in the top position.

Brush the grill with vegetable oil and grill the kebabs (or broil them on a rack set in a baking pan) for about 4 minutes on each side or until still pink in the middle. Serve with the mayonnaise.

NOTE: Swordfish or shark can be substituted.

Serves 4

grilled tuna with tahini parsley sauce

The first meal my mother-in-law prepared for me was the inspiration for this dish. Her tuna salad, drizzled with tahini dressing and topped with toasted pine nuts, caramelized onions, and parsley leaves, is still one of my favorites. The recipe was passed on to her from a Lebanese friend in Ohio. Some side dish possibilities are Grilled Ratatouille Salad (page 186) and Basmati Rice, Currant, and Carrot Salad (page 180).

FOR THE SAUCE

3 tablespoons stirred tahini (see Note)

2 tablespoons fresh lemon juice

½ teaspoon minced garlic

6 tablespoons water

6 tablespoons olive oil

¼ cup minced parsley

salt

freshly ground black pepper

1½ pounds fresh tuna steak (1 inch or thicker), cut into 4 portions

vegetable oil for brushing the tuna and grill

In a bowl, whisk together the sauce ingredients until smooth, and season with salt and pepper. Let the sauce stand at room temperature for at least 1 hour.

Trim away any dark meat from the tuna and brush all sides with oil. Season the steaks with salt and pepper.

Preheat a grill, or broiler with rack in the top position.

Brush the grill with oil and grill the tuna (or broil it on a rack set in a baking pan) for 3 minutes on each side.

Serve the tuna immediately with the room-temperature sauce.

NOTE: Tahini is a paste made from sesame seeds, and is available in most supermarkets. As it stands, the oil separates to the top (like fresh peanut butter), so the paste must be stirred to recombine it. Sometimes it is easier to stir with a fork, as the paste under the oil can be quite dense.

The sauce can be kept at room temperature for up to 8 hours, otherwise refrigerate it, covered, for up to 5 days. Bring to room temperature before serving.

Any other fish steak can be substituted.

Serves 4

tuna grilled korean-style

This aromatic marinade is used to flavor and tenderize beef in Korean cuisine. Do not marinate this longer than 2 hours, as the enzymes in ginger can over-tenderize the fish. Sweet-and-Sour Noodle and Cabbage Slaw (page 200) or Skinny Scalloped Potatoes (page 172) makes a nice accompaniment.

½ cup light soy sauce

2 tablespoons toasted sesame seed oil

1 teaspoon minced fresh ginger root

3 tablespoons sugar

1 tablespoon sesame seeds

3 garlic cloves, minced

¼ teaspoon salt

½ teaspoon freshly ground black pepper

1 ½ pounds tuna steak (1 inch or thicker),
  cut into 4 portions

In a plastic bag combine all ingredients except the tuna. Mix the marinade in the bag until combined and add the tuna, coating it completely. Seal the bag, refrigerate, and let the tuna marinate for 1 to 2 hours, turning it occasionally.

Preheat a grill, or broiler with rack in the top position.

Brush the grill with vegetable oil. Discard the marinade and grill the tuna (or broil it on a rack set in a baking pan) for 3 minutes on each side until medium rare.

Serve immediately.

NOTE: Swordfish or shark can also be prepared this way.

Serves 4

seared tuna with port and figs

This can definitely be put into your impressive entertainment file for special occasions, and your guests never have to know how simple it is. Suitable accompaniments include Peas and Rye Croutons (page 190), Watercress with Balsamic Vinegar and Butter (page 193), and Herbed Parmesan Grits (page 174).

½ onion, chopped

2 tablespoons olive oil

1½ cups tawny port wine

6 fresh thyme sprigs

½ cup undiluted canned beef consommé

½ cup dried figs, quartered

½ teaspoon cornstarch

1 teaspoon balsamic vinegar

2 pounds tuna steak (1 inch or thicker),
    cut into 4 portions

kosher or sea salt

freshly ground black pepper

vegetable oil

Cook the onion in the oil in a medium saucepan over low heat until softened. Add the port and 3 thyme sprigs and boil until it is reduced to ½ to ¾ cup liquid. Strain the mixture through a sieve set over a bowl, pressing hard on the solids. Return the liquid to the saucepan.

Add the consommé, the figs, and the remaining 3 thyme sprigs and simmer gently for 5 minutes. In a small cup, stir together the cornstarch and vinegar until smooth and whisk into the sauce. Simmer the sauce, stirring, for 2 minutes more, then remove from heat.

Season the tuna with salt and pepper and coat lightly with vegetable oil. Heat a heavy skillet over moderately high heat until very hot. Sear the tuna for about 3 minutes on each side to cook rare to medium rare.

Reheat the sauce while the tuna is cooking. Serve the tuna immediately, topped with the sauce.

NOTE: The sauce can be made 1 day in advance, kept covered and refrigerated.

Serves 4

grilled tuna marinated in carrot and basil sauce

In the great grilling countries of Argentina and Uruguay, beef is often served with a piquant sauce called *chimichurri*. A popular Argentine brand of chimichurri is made from shredded carrots, providing the inspiration for this marinade. The carrots cling to the tuna, forming a slight crust when grilled. Serve with Cucumber and Onion Salad with Yogurt Cumin Vinaigrette (page 202) and Zucchini Casserole (page 198).

½ cup finely shredded carrot

3 tablespoons fresh lemon juice

½ cup chopped fresh basil

½ cup vegetable oil

1 teaspoon dried oregano

1 teaspoon freshly ground black pepper

2 pounds tuna steak (1 inch or thicker),
    cut into 4 portions

In a shallow dish, stir together all of the ingredients except the tuna.

Add the tuna, coating it thoroughly, and let it marinate, covered and refrigerated, for 2 to 4 hours.

Preheat a grill, or broiler with rack in the top position.

Discard the marinade, letting some of the solids cling to the tuna. Brush the grill with vegetable oil and grill the tuna (or broil on a rack set in a baking pan) for 3 minutes on each side until medium rare.

Serve immediately.

NOTE: Any other fish steak can be substituted.

Serves 4

grilled tuna and peppers sandwich with herb mayonnaise

These casually elegant sandwiches make a perfect summer supper or luncheon. Make sure you use a fresh, high-quality bread. Grilled Ratatouille Salad (page 186) or Sautéed Fennel and Apples (page 189) makes a refreshing accompaniment.

⅓ cup mayonnaise (reduced-fat may be used)

¼ cup mixed minced herbs such as basil, cilantro, parsley, or chives

1 small garlic clove, minced

freshly ground black pepper

2 red, yellow, or orange bell peppers

1½ pounds tuna steak

8 slices from a round rustic country-style bread

vegetable oil

salt

In a small bowl, stir together the mayonnaise, herbs, garlic, and black pepper.

Quarter the bell peppers lengthwise, discarding the cores, and coat them with vegetable oil.

Preheat a grill, or broiler with rack in the top position.

Season the tuna with salt and pepper and grill the tuna and the peppers (or broil them on a rack set in a baking pan) for 3 to 4 minutes on each side until medium rare.

Slice the tuna across the grain and cut the peppers into strips. Spread the bread slices with the herb mayonnaise, and divide the tuna and the peppers among four of the slices. Top each sandwich with the remaining bread and cut it in half.

Makes 4 sandwiches

tuna roasted on leeks, potatoes, and sage

The bed of leeks and potatoes is like a potato pancake, but you don't have to worry about it falling apart—it's supposed to. Wateress with Balsamic Vinegar and Butter (page 198), Blasted Vegetables (page 188), or Braised Escarole with Tomatoes and Garlic (page 184) make this into a meal.

2 medium leeks, trimmed, washed well,
  and sliced thin (see Note)
3 tablespoons olive oil
2 tablespoons water
1 all-purpose potato (about ½ pound)
salt
freshly ground black pepper
2 teaspoons minced fresh sage leaves
2 pounds tuna steak, cut into 4 portions

Preheat the oven to 450°F.

In a large ovenproof skillet, cook the leeks in 2 tablespoons of oil and the water over moderate heat, stirring, for about 10 minutes, or until softened.

Peel the potato and grate it, using the large shredding holes of a four-sided grater. Stir the grated potato into the leeks and season the mixture with salt and pepper. Spread the mixture evenly in the pan, drizzle it with the remaining oil, and let it cook, undisturbed, over moderate heat for about 5 minutes or until the underside is golden.

With a spatula, turn the mixture over in sections and sprinkle with the sage leaves. Season the tuna with salt and pepper and arrange it on top of the vegetables.

Bake for 7 to 9 minutes or until the tuna is cooked through but still pink in the middle.

NOTE: Leeks are a treat, but a little grit can ruin an entire dish. Always wash them carefully. Trim the root ends and the tough dark green leaves. Split each leek lengthwise to within $\frac{1}{2}$ inch of the root end. With the leafy end hanging down, wash each leek under running water, separating each leaf to get out all the dirt.

Swordfish or halibut can be substituted for the tuna.

Serves 4

tuna in garlic caramel sauce

This dish was inspired by the delectable sauces served at my favorite Vietnamese restaurant. Caramel, garlic, and pepper may sound like a strange combination, but they join to create a most pleasing taste sensation. Serve this sophisticated entrée with rice and Watercress with Balsamic Vinegar and Butter (page 193) or Zesty Asparagus (page 192).

½ cup water

1½ tablespoons white wine vinegar

1 tablespoon soy sauce

1 teaspoon cornstarch

1 tablespoon butter

1 tablespoon minced garlic

3 tablespoons sugar

¾ teaspoon freshly ground coarse black pepper

2 pounds tuna steak, cut into 4 portions

1 tablespoon vegetable oil

salt

In a small bowl, stir together the water, vinegar, soy sauce, and cornstarch.

In a small nonstick skillet, combine the butter and garlic and heat over moderate heat until the butter is melted. Add the sugar and cook the mixture, stirring, until it is a pale peanut-butter color. Remove the skillet from the heat. Stir the liquid mixture to recombine and add to the skillet with the pepper. Return the skillet to the heat and cook the sauce, stirring, over low heat until the caramel is dissolved. Season with salt.

Rub the tuna with the oil and season with salt and pepper. Heat a large skillet over moderately high heat until it is very hot and add the tuna. Sear it for 3 minutes on each side or until it is nearly cooked through but there is still a band of red through the middle.

Spoon a puddle of the sauce onto each of four plates and lay the tuna on top. Serve any extra sauce separately.

Serves 4

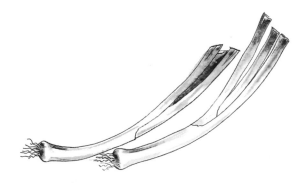

fresh tuna salad

For a taste of the good life, serve this refreshing salad on a bed of lettuce with a crusty peasant bread and a glass of wine. Ahh, simple pleasures.

½ cup dry white wine

½ cup water

½ teaspoon salt

¼ teaspoon black pepper

1 1¼ to 1½ pound tuna steak, trimmed of any dark flesh

3 tablespoons white wine vinegar

⅓ cup olive oil

½ cup pimiento-stuffed green olives, chopped

¼ cup minced scallions

½ cup chopped celery

2 tablespoons chopped pale green celery leaves

3 tablespoons minced fresh parsley

In a deep medium skillet, bring the wine and water to a boil. Add the salt, pepper, and tuna and poach it, covered, at a bare simmer, for about 10 minutes, or until just cooked through.

Transfer the tuna to a plate and boil the poaching liquid until reduced to 2 tablespoons. Transfer the liquid to a large bowl and whisk in the vinegar and oil, whisking until emulsified. Add the remaining ingredients and combine well.

Separate the tuna, along the grain, into large strips and add to the bowl. Stir gently and serve at room temperature.

NOTE: The salad can be made 1 day in advance, kept covered and refrigerated.

Serves 4

simple sides

Blasted Sweet Potatoes with Salt, Malt Vinegar, and Parsley

Old Bay Seasoned Roasted New Potatoes

Skinny Scalloped Potatoes

Herbed Parmesan Grits

Couscous with Dried Cranberries and Buttered Almonds

Toasted Vermicelli and Herbs

Egg Noodles with Tomato

Quick Rice and Beans

Fried Rice with Ham and Pineapple

Basmati Rice, Currant, and Carrot Salad

Mashed White Beans and Garlic

Charred Soy and Sesame String Beans

Braised Escarole with Tomatoes and Garlic

Cauliflower with Caramelized Onions and Poppy Seeds

Grilled Ratatouille Salad

Blasted Vegetables

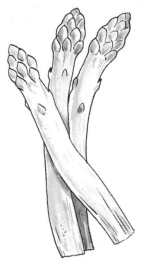

Sautéed Fennel and Apples

Peas and Rye Croutons

Fried Corn and Peppers with Butter and B[...]

Zesty Asparagus

Watercress with Balsamic Vinegar and Butter

Broiled Ripe Plantains

Gingered Spaghetti Squash

Zucchini Casserole

Sweet-and-Sour Noodle and Cabbage Slaw

Cucumber and Onion Salad with Yogurt Cumin Vinaigrette

Collard Greens with a Northern Accent

Green Salad with Grapes and Walnuts

Black Bean Salsa

Fresh Tomato Salsa

Pita Sticks

blasted sweet potatoes with salt, malt vinegar, and parsley

These sweet, salty, sour morsels are a lively change from the old baked potato.

2½ pounds sweet potatoes, peeled
3 tablespoons vegetable oil
2 tablespoons malt vinegar
1 teaspoon coarse kosher or sea salt
3 tablespoons minced fresh parsley
freshly ground black pepper

Preheat oven to 475°F.

Cut the sweet potatoes into ½-inch dice. In a large jelly-roll pan (or baking sheet with sides) toss the potato cubes with the oil until they are well coated.

Roast the potatoes in the oven, turning them occasionally, for 20 to 30 minutes. The potatoes will be tender long before they are crisp, so cook until they are deep golden but do not let them burn.

Transfer the potatoes to a bowl and toss with the vinegar. Add the salt, parsley, and pepper and toss. Serve immediately

Serves 4 to 6

old bay seasoned roasted new potatoes

Old Bay Seasoning is a commercial brand of shrimp or crab boil. Other seasoning mixes for seafood can be substituted, or other blends such as Cajun spices.

2 pounds red or white new potatoes (about 2 inches in diameter), scrubbed
1 tablespoon vegetable or olive oil
1 tablespoon Old Bay Seasoning

Preheat oven to 400°F.

Pat the potatoes dry and peel off a band of skin from around the middle of each. Toss the potatoes with the oil. Place them in a large jelly-roll pan or other shallow pan large enough to hold them in one layer. Sprinkle with the seasoning, shaking the pan to coat them evenly.

Roast the potatoes, turning occasionally, for 45 minutes or until browned and crisp.

NOTE: Larger potatoes can be substituted. Halve them or cut into quarters and cook in the same manner.

Serves 4

skinny scalloped potatoes

Scalloped potatoes are in my comfort-food hall of fame right next to macaroni and cheese. They only come out when my willpower is low and self-satisfaction wins over all commonsense rules of healthy eating. I came up with this slimmed-down version when I wanted to make the sinful classic but I only had 1 percent milk in the house.

2 pounds all-purpose potatoes (about 4 medium)
butter for coating the baking dish
3 cups skim, 1 percent, 2 percent, or whole milk
1 small onion, thinly sliced
1½ teaspoons fennel seeds (optional)
1 cup coarsely grated Parmesan or Swiss cheese
2 teaspoons salt
¼ teaspoon freshly ground black pepper

Preheat the oven to 350°F.

Peel and slice the potatoes about ¼ inch thick. Butter a shallow 2-quart baking dish.

In a large saucepan combine the milk, potatoes, onion, and fennel. Simmer the mixture, stirring gently, for 5 minutes. Transfer half the mixture to the buttered baking dish, and sprinkle half the cheese on top. Add the remaining potato mixture and top it with the remaining cheese.

Bake for 45 to 55 minutes or until the potatoes are tender and the top is browned. Let cool for at least 15 minutes before serving.

NOTE: This dish reheats very well and can be made a day in advance. Let cool, then cover and refrigerate. Reheat for 2 to 5 minutes in a microwave or 15 to 20 minutes in a 350°F oven.

Serves 8

herbed parmesan grits

These grits are an easy, white polenta. If you think you don't like grits, you haven't tried these!

3¾ cups water
½ teaspoon salt
¾ cup quick cooking grits
1 cup freshly grated Parmesan cheese
¾ cup minced parsley
½ teaspoon minced garlic
freshly ground black pepper
butter (optional)

Bring the water to a boil with the salt in a medium saucepan. Whisk in the grits and simmer the mixture, whisking constantly for 5 minutes. Remove the pan from the heat and stir in the Parmesan, parsley, garlic, and pepper.

Serve the grits with butter if desired.

Serves 4 to 6

couscous with dried cranberries and buttered almonds

Couscous is one of those foreign ingredients that sneaked into the American supermarket a few years ago and stayed. Its popularity can probably be attributed to its versatility and failure-proof ease of preparation. At the most, this dish takes 10 minutes to prepare.

2 cups canned chicken broth
⅔ cup dried cranberries (Craisins)
1½ cups couscous
2 tablespoons butter
½ cup sliced, chopped, or slivered almonds
chopped parsley or scallions for garnish (optional)
salt
freshly ground black pepper

In a small saucepan, combine the broth and cranberries and bring to a boil. Stir in the couscous, cover, and remove the pan from the heat.

In a small skillet, melt the butter over moderate heat and add the almonds. Cook, stirring, until they turn pale golden, about 3 minutes. Add to the couscous and toss to combine well.

Season couscous with pepper (be careful when adding salt, as the canned broth may be salty enough). Add parsley or scallions if desired.

Serves 4

toasted vermicelli and herbs

Here is a simple way to make pasta unusual. The dry noodles are fried in a skillet and cooked slowly in liquid until it is all absorbed, like rice. This makes a great side dish for nearly any meal, and kids love it.

½ pound vermicelli or thin spaghetti
2 tablespoons olive oil
1 small garlic clove, minced
1¼ cups chicken broth
1 cup water
¾ cup mixed chopped fresh herbs such as parsley, basil, chives, and thyme
salt
freshly ground black pepper

Break the pasta into 2-inch lengths. In a large skillet with a lid, brown it in the oil over moderate heat, stirring, but do not let it burn. Add the garlic and cook, stirring, for 1 minute.

Add the broth and water and simmer the mixture, covered, stirring occasionally, for 10 minutes, or until the pasta is tender. The pasta should be slightly saucy. Add more water if it seems too dry.

Stir in the herbs and season with salt and pepper.

Serves 4

egg noodles with tomato

This simple side dish is best when made with summer tomatoes at their peak. Using any pasta, this can become a satisfying vegetarian main course with basil and cubed fresh mozzarella added.

1 large tomato, diced

½ cup chopped onion, preferably Vidalia, Oso, Maui, or another sweet onion

¼ cup olive oil

12 ounces wide egg noodles

salt

freshly ground black pepper

In a large bowl, stir together the tomato, onion, and oil.

In a pot of boiling salted water, cook the noodles until just tender. Drain the noodles, add them to the tomato mixture, and toss well. Season with salt and pepper.

Serves 4

quick rice and beans

Beans and rice are everyday fare in cultures around the world, and with good reason. Legumes, which are high in protein, iron, and vitamins, mixed with rice, which has all the nutritional elements beans are missing, combine to make the perfect food. Man *can* live on rice and beans, (unlike bread) alone! Here is a way to enjoy a Cuban favorite, black beans and rice, without the hours of cooking required by the traditional method of preparation.

1 small onion, chopped
½ green bell pepper, chopped (about ½ cup)
1 tablespoon olive oil
1 15½-ounce can black beans, drained
½ cup water
½ teaspoon ground cumin
½ teaspoon dried oregano
1 tablespoon tomato paste
salt
freshly ground black pepper
4½ cups long-grain white rice, cooked (1½ cups uncooked)

In a saucepan, cook the onion and bell pepper in oil over moderate heat, stirring, until softened. Add the remaining ingredients except the rice and simmer, stirring occasionally, for 15 minutes.

To serve, spoon the rice separately onto a plate and top it with the beans.

Serves 4

fried rice with ham and pineapple

2¾ cups water

1 teaspoon salt

1½ cups long-grain white rice

1 small onion, chopped

1 garlic clove, minced

2 tablespoons vegetable oil

1¼ cups chopped baked ham

1 8-ounce can pineapple chunks, drained

1 tablespoon soy sauce

salt

freshly ground black pepper

chopped scallions and/or peanuts for garnish (optional)

In a large saucepan, bring the water to a boil with the salt; add the rice. Simmer the rice, covered, for 20 minutes or until the water is absorbed, and fluff it with a fork.

While the rice is cooking, sauté the onion and garlic in the oil in a large nonstick skillet over moderately low heat until softened. Add the ham and cook over moderate heat until the mixture begins to turn golden. Add the pineapple, breaking up the pieces slightly, and cook 5 minutes more.

Add the cooked rice to the skillet. Stir in the soy sauce, salt, and pepper. Turn the mixture with a spatula over moderate heat for about 5 minutes or until the rice is lightly browned in spots. Garnish with the scallions and peanuts if desired.

Serves 4

basmati rice, currant, and carrot salad

Fragrant rice with earthy cardamom and sweet/tart flavors may sound exotic, but it is a versatile accompaniment to all types of fish, meat, and poultry. I first tasted this delicious combination with Afghan shish kebabs, served hot as a pilaf without the oil.

1 cup Basmati, jasmine, or other extra-long-grain rice (see Note)
1¾ cups water
1 teaspoon salt
½ teaspoon ground cardamom
⅓ cup dried currants or raisins
1 cup finely chopped carrot
⅓ cup chopped onion or scallions
¼ cup rice vinegar
¼ cup vegetable oil
freshly ground black pepper

Rinse the rice in a sieve under cold water until it runs clear.

Put the rice in a saucepan with the water, salt, cardamom, and currants; bring to a rolling boil. Reduce the heat and simmer, covered, for 15 minutes. Fluff the rice with a fork and transfer it to a bowl to cool. Add the remaining ingredients and toss. Season with salt and pepper. Serve the salad at room temperature or chilled.

NOTE: Basmati is a fragrant long-grain rice often imported from India. Some American-grown varieties are Texamati, Wehani, and Wild Pecan Rice (which doesn't contain nuts). Jasmine is a fragrant long-grain rice used in Thai cuisine. Both are becoming more available in supermarkets' gourmet sections. If you cannot find it, ask your grocer (they are sometimes shelved in unexpected places) or use regular long-grain rice instead.

This dish can also be served warm as a pilaf, omitting the oil and vinegar.

The salad can be made 1 day in advance, kept covered and refrigerated.

Serves 4

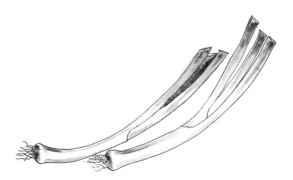

mashed white beans and garlic

This substitute for mashed potatoes is equally comforting and it's a tasty way to absorb extra juices from a saucy dish.

1 19-ounce can white navy or cannellini beans
2 large garlic cloves, minced
2 tablespoons olive oil
½ cup chicken broth or water
freshly ground black pepper
salt (optional)

Drain the beans in a colander and rinse well.

In a saucepan, cook the garlic in oil over moderately low heat until softened, about 5 minutes. Add the broth and beans and simmer for 5 minutes. Mash the mixture with a potato masher or transfer to a food processor and puree until just smooth. Season with pepper (and salt, if needed, but remember that canned beans and broth can be salty).

Serves 4

charred soy and sesame string beans

Turn your exhaust fan on high for this one. It gets the kitchen pretty smoky, but it's worth it. Make this ahead of time and reheat if you are having company.

1 tablespoon vegetable oil
1 pound green beans, rinsed, dried, and trimmed
1 teaspoon sesame seeds
3 tablespoons soy sauce
kosher or sea salt
freshly ground black pepper

In a nonstick skillet, heat the oil over high heat until hot but not smoking. Sauté the beans, covered, turning them with tongs every minute, for 5 minutes or until tender and browned in spots. Stir in the sesame seeds and cook, uncovered, 1 minute more.

Remove the pan from heat and add the soy sauce (it will boil rapidly), tossing the beans until coated well. Season with salt and pepper.

Serves 4

braised escarole with tomatoes and garlic

Escarole looks like a tough head of lettuce with broad leaves and white stems. Whenever it appears in the market I grab it to make this dish.

1 1-pound head escarole
2 garlic cloves, minced
1 tablespoon olive oil
1 1-pound can whole tomatoes, including the liquid
kosher or sea salt
freshly ground black pepper

Tear the escarole into large pieces. Wash well and spin dry.

In a large deep skillet, cook the garlic in oil over low heat, stirring, until pale golden. Add the escarole and tomatoes, crushing them. Simmer the mixture, stirring occasionally, about 5 minutes or until the escarole is just tender but still slightly crisp. Season with salt and pepper.

NOTE: This dish is best served immediately, but it can be made up to 2 hours in advance and kept in the skillet, off the heat. Reheat quickly over moderately high heat.

Serves 4

cauliflower with caramelized onions and poppy seeds

The sweet golden onions blend with the crunchy poppy seeds to make plain cauliflower shine.

1 medium head cauliflower (about 1½ pounds), trimmed and halved

3 cups coarsely chopped onion

3 tablespoons olive oil

1 tablespoon poppy seeds

1 tablespoon butter

1 tablespoon lemon juice

salt

freshly ground black pepper

Bring 1 inch of water to a boil in a large saucepan and add the cauliflower, stem ends down. Cover and steam over high heat for about 3 minutes or until just tender but still slightly crisp. Drain and separate into bite-sized pieces.

In a nonstick skillet, cook the onion in the oil over moderately high heat, stirring, until golden. Add the poppy seeds and the butter and cook 2 minutes more. Add the lemon juice and cauliflower, and stir until the cauliflower is reheated. Season well with salt and pepper.

Serves 4

grilled ratatouille salad

A great addition to an alfresco meal, this can be grilled in advance and left at room temperature while the main course is being prepared, or it can be refrigerated and served chilled.

1½ to 2 pounds eggplant

1 pound zucchini or yellow squash, scrubbed

1 large sweet onion

2 tablespoons vegetable oil

2 tablespoons balsamic vinegar

1½ cups diced fresh tomato

2 tablespoons capers

salt

freshly ground black pepper

¼ cup chopped fresh basil or parsley

I prefer to leave the eggplant skin on, but it can be peeled if desired. Cut the eggplant into 1-inch-thick rounds. Halve the zucchini lengthwise. Peel the onion but do not trim the ends, and cut it lengthwise (through the ends) into ¾-inch-thick slices.

Whisk together the oil and 1 tablespoon of the vinegar and brush it on the vegetables, coating them well.

Preheat a grill, or broiler with rack in the top position.

Grill the vegetables (or broil them on a rack set in a baking pan), turning them often, for about 10 to 15 minutes or until they are tender but still hold their shape.

Cut eggplant into large cubes. Cut zucchini crosswise into thick slices. Trim and chop the onion slices. Toss the vegetables together with the tomato, capers, remaining 1 tablespoon vinegar, salt, pepper, and basil or parsley.

Serves 4 to 6

blasted vegetables

This bold method—quickly blasting vegetables in a hot oven, just long enough to lock in their fresh taste and become tender and lightly browned—yields satisfying results. Certainly you can add chopped herbs, grated zest, or other flavors at the end, but salt and pepper are all I need to crown this dish.

1 pound snow or sugar snap peas, green beans, asparagus, or cauliflower florets, rinsed and drained

1 tablespoon vegetable oil

kosher salt

freshly ground black pepper

Preheat the oven to 450°F.

In a jelly-roll pan or cookie sheet with sides, drizzle the vegetables with the oil and toss them to coat well. Spread the vegetables in a single layer in the pan and bake in the middle of the oven for 5 minutes or until they are tender and browned in spots.

Season the vegetables with salt and pepper and transfer to a serving dish.

Serves 4

sautéed fennel and apples

This delicate and unusual side dish is a welcome accompaniment to any fall or winter dish, when both ingredients are at their peak.

1 large fennel bulb (see Note)
1 Granny Smith apple
1 tablespoon butter
salt
freshly ground black pepper

Halve the fennel bulb and trim out the tough core from the bottom of the bulb. Slice it very thinly crosswise. Reserve the feathery fennel tops. (They look like fresh dill.)

Peel the apple and cut it into $\frac{1}{4}$-inch-thick sticks.

In a medium skillet, cook the fennel in the butter over moderate heat, stirring, about 5 minutes or until tender, but still slightly crisp. Add the apple and stir, gently, until the apple is just heated through. (Do not overcook or the apple will fall apart.) Chop the reserved fennel tops and stir about 2 tablespoons into the fennel. Season with salt and pepper.

NOTE: Fennel is a vegetable that looks like celery with a big bulb at the end and tops that look like feathery fresh dill. It is often mislabeled as anise in markets, perhaps because of their similar licorice flavors. Every part of the fennel plant is edible, and it's delicious whether raw, sautéed, braised, or grilled.

Serves 4

peas and rye croutons

This is a supersimple side dish, which gives an old standby some pizzazz.

4 slices rye bread with seeds
3 tablespoons butter
salt
freshly ground black pepper
3½ cups frozen peas
2 teaspoons yellow mustard seeds
1 cup water

Cut the rye bread into ¼-inch squares. There should be about 2½ cups.

In a medium skillet melt the butter over moderate heat and add the bread cubes. Cook the croutons, tossing often to keep them from burning, for about 10 minutes or until they are golden and crisp. Remove the skillet from the heat and season the croutons generously with salt and pepper.

In a saucepan combine the peas, mustard seeds, and water. Boil the mixture until the peas are tender, about 5 minutes. Drain well in a sieve. When ready to serve, add the peas to the skillet with the croutons and heat the mixture over moderate heat, stirring, until hot.

NOTE: The croutons can be made 2 days in advance, kept in an airtight container at room temperature.

Serves 4

fried corn and peppers with butter and basil

Lightly browning corn in this manner gives it a slight roasted flavor. A little heavy cream can be added at the end if you have a hankering for a luscious creamed-corn taste.

2 cups fresh or frozen corn kernels
1 large red bell pepper, chopped
1 tablespoon butter
1 tablespoon chopped fresh basil or parsley
salt
freshly ground black pepper

In a nonstick skillet, cook corn and peppers in butter over moderately high heat, stirring occasionally, until the vegetables are pale golden, about 15 minutes. Stir in the basil and season with salt and pepper.

NOTE: This dish can be kept covered and refrigerated for up to 2 days. Reheat in a skillet over low heat, adding a little water if necessary to moisten.

Serves 4

zesty asparagus

This is a change from steaming whole spears of asparagus and lining them up on a plate. With this method it is easier to judge when the asparagus is done, to keep from overcooking.

1 pound asparagus, tough ends trimmed
1 tablespoon butter
freshly grated zest from 1 lemon (see Note)
2 tablespoons finely chopped celery leaves
salt
freshly ground black pepper

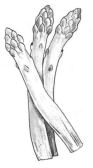

Cut the asparagus at an angle into 1-inch pieces. In a large skillet, heat the butter over moderately high heat, add the asparagus, and cook, stirring, for 3 to 5 minutes or until tender but still crisp. Add the zest, celery leaves, salt, and pepper.

NOTE: Be sure not to include any of the bitter white pith when grating any citrus zest. Only the thin outer yellow layer has the desirable intense lemon flavor and oils. Your lemon should still be slightly yellow after grating.

Serves 4

watercress with balsamic vinegar and butter

This recipe is good with many kinds of greens. If you are lucky enough to have access to field cress, thicker and leafier than watercress, substitute it in this recipe. I got hooked on it when in early spring it appeared in crisp, rinsed mounds in the greens section of my supermarket. Unfortunately I haven't seen it since. Farmers' markets are a good place to look.

¼ cup balsamic vinegar

2 tablespoons butter

1½ teaspoons sugar

1½ pounds watercress, beet greens, or spinach,
    washed well, with coarse stems discarded

salt

freshly ground black pepper

In a large saucepan, boil the vinegar until it is reduced by half (2 tablespoons). Add the butter, sugar, and greens. Cook the mixture over low heat, stirring, for 10 minutes or until tender. Season with salt and pepper.

Serves 4

broiled ripe plantains

Serve these with nearly any main course and watch them disappear.

3 ripe (the skin should be brownish black) plantains
3 tablespoons melted butter
salt
freshly ground black pepper

Preheat the broiler, with a rack placed closest to the heat.

To peel plantains: Trim the ends and with the tip of a paring knife, slit the skin lengthwise. Pry the skin from the plantain.

Slice each plantain diagonally, about ½ inch thick, and arrange in a single layer on a jelly-roll pan or baking sheet with sides. Brush both sides of the slices with the butter and sprinkle with salt and pepper.

Broil the plantains for 8 to 10 minutes or until they are browned. Turn them and broil about 5 minutes on the other side or until browned. Transfer the plantains to a heatproof platter and keep in a warm oven, uncovered, until ready to serve.

NOTE: Plantains resemble big, bruised, thick-skinned, bad-looking bananas. They range from green (unripe) to yellow (half ripe) to black (ripe), and even at their ripest are still firm and less sweet than you would expect from a banana. There are different methods of preparation for different stages of ripeness. Think of them as a vegetable, starchy like the versatile potato, not to be eaten raw, but fried or added to stews. Store at room temperature and they will keep for a long time, ripening slowly.

Serves 4

gingered spaghetti squash

Unfortunately my family does not like winter squash, one of my favorites. However, this dish was a big hit. In defense of his still unchanged aversion, my husband remarked, "Well, it's not really squash."

1 2-pound spaghetti squash
2 tablespoons butter
1 2-inch piece of fresh ginger
salt
freshly ground black pepper
½ cup chopped parsley

Preheat oven to 350°F.

Halve the squash and scrape out the seeds and loose strands. Arrange the squash in a large baking dish, cut sides down. Add ½ inch of water to the dish and cover it with foil. Bake the squash 45 minutes or until it is slightly soft when pressed.

With a fork, scrape the stringy flesh into a bowl. Toss the shreds with the butter.

Shred the ginger with the coarse side of a four-sided grater. Put small amounts of ginger into a garlic press and squeeze the liquid over the squash, discarding the solids. Stir in the salt, pepper, and parsley.

NOTE: The spaghetti squash can be cooked in a microwave oven. Place in a microwave-safe dish, cover with plastic wrap, and cook at high power for 15 to 20 minutes.

The cooked squash can be transferred to a baking dish and topped with grated white cheddar or crumbled mild goat cheese. Bake at 350°F for about 20 minutes or until the squash is hot and the cheese is melted.

Serves 4

zucchini casserole

This old-fashioned vegetable dish is still a favorite and a great way to use up a large summer crop of squash.

1 small onion, chopped
1 large garlic clove, minced
2 tablespoons butter
1 pound zucchini or yellow squash, scrubbed and sliced thin
1½ tablespoons all-purpose flour
¾ cup milk (whole, low-fat, or skim)
½ cup grated Parmesan cheese
¾ cup fresh bread crumbs
1 tablespoon chopped fresh basil, or 1 teaspoon dried
salt
freshly ground black pepper

Preheat the oven to 350°F.

In a large skillet, cook the onion and garlic in the butter over moderate heat, stirring, until softened. Add the zucchini and cook it over moderately high heat, stirring, for about 3 minutes, until it begins to get tender. Reduce the heat to low and add the flour, stirring until it is incorporated.

Remove the pan from the heat and stir in the milk, Parmesan, ½ cup of the bread crumbs, basil, salt, and pepper. Transfer the mixture to a 9-inch pie dish or other shallow baking dish and sprinkle the top with the remaining ¼ cup bread crumbs.

Bake for 25 to 30 minutes or until it is bubbling in the middle and pale golden on top.

NOTE: The casserole can be made 1 day in advance, kept covered and refrigerated. Reheat, uncovered, in a microwave or in a 350°F oven.

Serves 6

sweet-and-sour noodle and cabbage slaw

This nonfat slaw is a jumble of fresh flavors and textures, inspired by the cuisines of Southeast Asia. It is colorful and versatile, appropriate for formal dinner parties as well as summertime picnics.

⅓ cup lime or lemon juice

1 tablespoon sugar

1 tablespoon minced peeled fresh ginger root

⅛ to ¼ teaspoon cayenne pepper

2 teaspoons salt

2 tablespoons water

5 cups finely shredded cabbage (about ½ small head)

2 red bell peppers, cut into fine strips

½ cup thinly sliced scallion

½ cup roughly chopped fresh mint

½ cup roughly chopped fresh basil

¼ cup roughly chopped cilantro

¼ pound dried angel hair pasta or thin spaghetti

In a large bowl, whisk together the lime juice, sugar, ginger, cayenne, salt, and water. Add the cabbage, peppers, scallion, mint, basil, and cilantro; toss well.

In a large pot of boiling salted water, cook the pasta until just tender. Rinse briefly under cold water and drain well. Add to cabbage mixture and toss. Slaw can be served at room temperature or cold.

NOTE: The slaw can be made 8 hours in advance, kept covered and refrigerated.

Serves 6

cucumber and onion salad with yogurt cumin vinaigrette

This versatile side dish can be paired up with hot dogs, hamburgers, pot roasts, and all kinds of fish. My Cuban friends have adopted this as an accompaniment to their roast pork and boiled yuca.

2 cucumbers (about 1 pound), peeled and very thinly sliced

½ red onion, thinly sliced

2 teaspoons salt

½ cup plain yogurt

¾ teaspoon ground cumin

2 tablespoons olive oil

2 teaspoons lemon juice

¼ cup chopped fresh parsley, cilantro, basil, or mint

freshly ground black pepper to taste

In a large bowl toss together the cucumbers, onion, and salt. Add cold water to cover the mixture by 1 inch and refrigerate for 30 minutes.

Drain the vegetables, pressing out as much water as possible, and return them to the bowl. Stir in the remaining ingredients and refrigerate the salad until ready to serve.

NOTE: The salad can be made 8 hours in advance, kept covered and refrigerated.

Whole milk yogurt tastes the best here. Low-fat yogurt is okay to use, but nonfat yogurt produces a chalky, insipid flavor, hardly worth the savings in calories.

Serves 4 to 6

collard greens with a northern accent

Collard greens are no longer just a southern dish. They are available everywhere and gaining popularity for their nutritional benefits and distinct flavor. I like to cook them with sweet and sour flavors to balance their bitterness.

1 pound collard greens or kale

½ pound sweet or hot Italian sausage (about 2 links),
   or 4 slices bacon, chopped into ½-inch pieces

1 cup apple cider or juice

2 tablespoons wine or cider vinegar

salt

freshly ground black pepper

Wash the greens well and with a paring knife, cut out the tough center vein from each leaf. Stack the leaves and cut them into ½-inch-wide strips.

Squeeze the sausage from the casings into a large deep skillet or saucepan and cook it (or the bacon) over moderate heat, breaking up the meat, until it is no longer pink. Add the cider, vinegar, and greens. Simmer the greens, covered, stirring occasionally, for 50 minutes to 1 hour, or until they are tender. Season with salt and pepper.

Serves 4

green salad with grapes and walnuts

This light, refreshing salad is equally delicious made with spinach. Create a main course by adding cooked shrimp, salmon, or tuna.

6 tablespoons vegetable oil

2 tablespoons white or red wine vinegar

1 teaspoon honey

salt

freshly ground black pepper

1 cup seedless red grapes, halved

⅔ cup coarsely chopped walnuts

6 to 8 cups torn romaine, red leaf, or Boston lettuce, washed and dried

In a serving bowl, whisk together the oil, vinegar, honey, salt, and pepper. Stir in the grapes and walnuts. Add the lettuce, toss well, and serve immediately.

NOTE: If a nuttier flavor is desired, toast the walnuts lightly in a 350°F oven for about 8 minutes. Be careful not to burn them or they become bitter.

The dressing can be made 1 day in advance. Keep it covered and refrigerated.

Serves 4 to 6

black bean salsa

Salsas go particularly well with fish. They are perfect condiments to spruce up an ordinary grilled fish steak.

2 cups canned black beans, rinsed and drained

¾ cup chopped onion

2 small hot chilis (or to taste; see page 61), such as jalapeño or serrano, seeded and minced, or jalapeño hot sauce to taste

3 tablespoons chopped fresh cilantro

3 tablespoons fresh lime juice

½ teaspoon ground cumin

In a bowl, stir together all the ingredients. Refrigerate, covered, stirring occasionally, for 30 minutes to 4 hours.

NOTE: This salsa is best eaten fresh. The flavors start to fade after a day.

Makes 2½ cups

fresh tomato salsa

2½ cups chopped fresh tomatoes

½ cup finely chopped green bell
    pepper or other sweet pepper

¾ cup finely chopped celery

½ cup finely chopped onion

1 garlic clove, minced

1 tablespoon red wine vinegar

2 tablespoons finely chopped fresh cilantro

salt

freshly ground black pepper

In a bowl, stir together all the ingredients. Keep salsa covered and refrigerated for at least 1 hour and up to 2 days.

Makes about 3½ cups

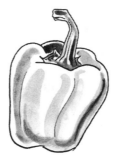

pita sticks

These add a nice crunch to appetizers and salads. An appealing presentation is to stand them on end in a large mug or jar.

4 6-inch pita pockets
2 tablespoons olive oil
1 teaspoon kosher or sea salt

Preheat oven to 400°F.

Cut the pitas into ½-inch-wide strips and arrange in a jelly-roll pan or baking sheet with sides. Drizzle with the oil and sprinkle with salt.

Bake the sticks for 5 to 8 minutes or until golden and crisp.

Index

almonds:
  in baked shrimp pesto, 30–31
  buttered, couscous with dried cranberries and, 175
  shrimp stuffed with pita, spinach, sun-dried tomatoes and, 34–35
appetizers:
  Asian-style salmon lettuce rolls, 104–5
  cilantro shrimp with peanut dip, 6–7
  cornmeal fried shrimp, 47
  grilled shrimp wrapped in hot cappicola and basil, 16–17
  a new shrimp cocktail, 3
  pickled shrimp with wasabi, 12–13
  pita sticks, 208
  sautéed shrimp with black bean sauce, 14–15
  tsatsiki shrimp salad, 32
apples, sautéed fennel and, 189
apricots, salmon baked with water chestnuts and, 89
artichoke heart:
  Caesar shrimp, and tomato kebabs, 22–23
  and shrimp fettuccini Alfredo, 40–41

Asian-style salmon lettuce rolls, 104–5
asparagus:
  in blasted vegetables, 188
  and chickpea vinaigrette, sautéed salmon with, 72–73
  zesty, 192
avocado(s):
  in Asian-style salmon lettuce rolls, 104–5
  in salmon cobb salad with creamy mustard dressing, 102–3
  shrimp, and jicama salad with cumin grapefruit dressing, 4–5
bacon:
  in salmon cobb salad with creamy mustard dressing, 102–3
  shrimp with broccoli rabe, pasta and, 42–43
  spinach, crispy salmon on tangerine and, 62–63
baked, xvii

  halibut Georgiana, 120–21
  salmon with bell pepper salsa, 82
  shrimp pesto, 30–31
basil:
  in baked shrimp pesto, 30–31

and carrot sauce, grilled tuna marinated in, 158–59
corn broth, halibut in, 128–29
fried corn and peppers with butter and, 191
in grilled salmon steaks on citrus, 66–67
grilled shrimp wrapped in hot cappicola and, 16–17
in sautéed salmon smothered in summer (tomatoes and basil), 80–81
Basmati rice, currant, and carrot salad, 180–81
beans:
  garlic and mashed white, 182
  quick rice and, 178
beet greens:
  with balsamic vinegar and butter, 193
  shrimp with bacon, pasta and, 42–43
beets, halibut with, 130–31
bell pepper(s):
  in deviled shrimp, 48–49
  and fried corn with butter and basil, 191
  and grilled tuna sandwich with herb mayonnaise, 160–61

bell pepper(s): (*cont.*)
  in a new shrimp cocktail,
    3
  salsa, baked salmon with,
    82
  yellow, and salmon
    chowder, 110–11
Big-Easy shrimp, 26–27
black bean:
  salsa, 206
  sauce, sautéed shrimp
    with, 14–15
blackened salmon on zesty
  cabbage, 74–75
blasted:
  sweet potatoes with salt,
    malt vinegar, and
    parsley, 170
  vegetables, 188
boiled, xvii
  shrimp, simply, 2
braised escarole with
  tomatoes and garlic, 184
broccoli, stir-fried shrimp
  and, 28–29
broccoli rabe, shrimp with
  bacon, pasta and, 42–43
broiled, xvii
  ripe plantains, 194–95
broth:
  halibut in basil corn,
    128–29
  salmon poached in lemon
    tomato, 96–97
Buffalo shrimp, 8–9
  dip, 9
buying seafood, x-xi

cabbage:
  and noodle slaw, sweet-
    and-sour, 200–201
  zesty, blackened salmon
    on, 74–75
Caesar shrimp, tomato, and
  artichoke heart kebabs,
    22–23
capers:
  in deviled shrimp, 48–49

  in roasted salmon
    puttanesca, 83
  in salmon baked with
    deviled egg sauce,
    90–91
cappicola, hot, grilled
  shrimp wrapped in
  basil and, 16–17
carrot(s):
  and basil sauce, grilled
    tuna marinated in,
    158–59
  Basmati rice, and currant
    salad, 180–81
  and pineapple salsa,
    curried swordfish
    kebabs with, 138–39
casserole, zucchini, 198–99
cauliflower:
  in blasted vegetables,
    188
  with caramelized onions
    and poppy seeds, 185
celery, salmon poached in
  sake with ginger and,
    94
charred soy and sesame
  green beans, 183
chickpea and asparagus
  vinaigrette, sautéed
  salmon with, 72–73
chili-rubbed halibut with
  Mexican pickled onions,
    114–15
chilis, *see* jalapeño pepper(s)
chive(s):
  mayonnaise, grilled
    lemon-pepper tuna
    kebabs with, 150–51
  sour cream sauce, potato-
    crusted halibut with,
    116–17
chowder, salmon and yellow
  pepper, 110–11
chutney:
  mint, grilled tandoori-
    style shrimp with, 18–19
  sauce, sweet, hot, and
    sour, 53

cilantro:
  in grilled salmon with
    green chili coconut
    sauce, 68–69
  shrimp with peanut dip,
    6–7
coconut:
  graham shrimp, crisp,
    52–53
  green chili sauce, grilled
    salmon with, 68–69
collard greens with a
  northern accent, 204
corn:
  basil broth, halibut in,
    128–29
  and peppers with butter
    and basil, fried, 191
cornmeal fried shrimp, 47
couscous with dried
  cranberries and
  buttered almonds, 175
cranberries:
  couscous with buttered
    almonds and dried, 175
  in salmon in mock
    tamarind sauce, 100–101
crisp(y):
  coconut graham shrimp,
    52–53
  salmon on lentils with
    fried onions, 78–79
  salmon on tangerine and
    bacon spinach, 62–63
  sesame shrimp, 50–51
croutons, peas and rye, 190
cucumber:
  and onion salad with
    yogurt cumin
    vinaigrette, 202–3
  salsa, gingered, orange-
    glazed shrimp with,
    20–21
  in tsatsiki shrimp salad,
    32
  -yogurt sauce with
    poached salmon, 108–9
currant, Basmati rice, and
  carrot salad, 180–81

curried shrimp with sweet
onions, 46
curried swordfish kebabs
with pineapple and
carrot salsa, 138–39
deveining shrimp, xii-xiii
deviled shrimp, 48–49
dressings:
for Buffalo shrimp, 9
creamy mustard, salmon
cobb salad with, 102–3
cumin grapefruit, shrimp,
jicama, and avocado
salad with, 4–5
peanut dip, cilantro
shrimp with, 6–7
see also vinaigrettes

eggplant, in grilled
ratatouille salad, 186–87
eggs:
salmon baked with
deviled-egg sauce,
90–91
in salmon cobb salad with
creamy mustard
dressing, 102–3
escarole, braised, with
tomatoes and garlic, 184

fajitas, grilled margarita
shrimp, 10–11
fennel:
and apples, sautéed, 189
and salmon under wraps,
92–93
figs, seared tuna with port
and, 156–57
fish steaks, *see specific fish*
fresh tomato salsa, 207
fried, xvii
corn and peppers with
butter and basil, 191
rice with ham and
pineapple, 179

garlic:
braised escarole with
tomatoes and, 184

caramel sauce, tuna in,
164–65
mashed white beans and,
182
ginger(ed):
cucumber salsa with
orange-glazed shrimp,
20–21
salmon poached in sake
with celery and, 94
spaghetti squash, 196–97
grape(s):
green salad with walnuts
and, 205
sauce, salmon in, 98–99
grapefruit, in grilled salmon
steaks on citrus, 66–67
green beans:
in blasted vegetables, 188
charred soy and sesame,
183
green chili:
cream, salmon in, 70–71
see also jalapeño pepper(s)
green salad with grapes and
walnuts, 205
grilled, xvii
butterflied shrimp with
pineapple scallion-
butter sauce, 24–25
lemon-pepper tuna
kebabs with chive
mayonnaise, 150–51
margarita shrimp fajitas,
10–11
molasses salmon with
lime, 64
ratatouille salad, 186–87
salmon steaks on citrus,
66–67
salmon with green chili
coconut sauce, 68–69
sangria swordfish, 148–49
shrimp wrapped in hot
cappicola and basil,
16–17
swordfish Dijon, 147
swordfish in flank steak
marinade, 137
tandoori-style shrimp

with mint chutney,
18–19
tuna and peppers
sandwich with herb
mayonnaise, 160–61
tuna marinated in carrot
and basil sauce, 158–59
tuna with tahini parsley
sauce, 152–53
grits, herbed Parmesan,
174

halibut, xiv
baked, Georgiana, 120–21
in basil corn broth,
128–29
with beets, 130–31
chili-rubbed, with
Mexican pickled onions,
114–15
in curried pumpkin sauce
with sunflower and
pomegranate seeds,
142–43
grilled, *see* halibut, grilled
in lemon sauce, 126
marinade, 58–59
marmalade-marinated,
140–41
and mushroom Marsala,
144–45
nut-crusted, 127
with onions, raisins, and
pine nuts, 132–33
poached in curried
tomato sauce, 134–35
potato-crusted, with chive
sour cream sauce,
116–17
roasted, Cuban-style, 136
roasted, with onion wine
sauce, 118–19
roasted on leeks, potatoes,
and sage, 162–63
sesame-crusted, teriyaki,
58–59
steak baked with roasted
jalapeño tartar sauce,
122–23

halibut: (*cont.*)
    stewed with tomatoes
        and white beans,
        124–25
halibut, grilled:
    Dijon, 147
    in flank steak marinade,
        137
    marinated in basil and
        carrot sauce, 158–59
    molasses, with lime, 64
    sangria, 148–49
    with tahini parsley sauce,
        152–53
ham, fried rice with
    pineapple and, 179
herbed Parmesan grits,
    174
hors d'oeuvres, *see*
    appetizers
horseradish:
    in a new shrimp cocktail,
        3
    salmon pie with roasted
        peppers, leeks and,
        86–87

jalapeño pepper(s):
    in black bean salsa,
        206
    in grilled salmon with
        green chili coconut
        sauce, 68–69
    in jerk-spiced salmon
        steaks, 60–61
    tartar sauce, roasted,
        halibut steak baked
        with, 122–23
jerk-spiced salmon steaks,
    60–61
jicama, shrimp, and avocado
    salad with cumin
    grapefruit dressing, 4–5

kale:
    with a northern accent,
        204
    shrimp with bacon, pasta
        and, 42–43

kebabs:
    Caesar shrimp, tomato,
        and artichoke heart,
        22–23
    curried swordfish, with
        pineapple and carrot
        salsa, 138–39
    grilled lemon-pepper
        tuna, with chive
        mayonnaise, 150–51

leeks:
    salmon pie with roasted
        peppers, horseradish
        and, 86–87
    tuna roasted on potatoes,
        sage and, 162–63
lemon:
    in grilled salmon steaks
        on citrus, 66–67
    tomato broth, salmon
        poached in, 96–97
lentils, crisp salmon on,
    with fried onions, 78–79
lettuce rolls, Asian-style
    salmon, 104–5
lime:
    grilled molasses salmon
        with, 64
    in grilled salmon steaks
        on citrus, 66–67

marinades:
    for Caesar shrimp, tomato,
        and artichoke heart
        kebabs, 22–23
    carrot and basil sauce,
        grilled tuna marinated
        in, 158–59
    flank steak, grilled
        swordfish in, 137
    for grilled margarita
        shrimp fajitas, 10–11
    for grilled sangria
        swordfish, 148–49
    marmalade-marinated
        swordfish, 140–41
    for pickled shrimp with
        wasabi, 12–13

    for sesame-crusted
        salmon teriyaki,
        58–59
marmalade-marinated
    swordfish, 140–41
mashed white beans and
    -garlic, 182
mayonnaise:
    in Buffalo shrimp dip, 9
    chive, grilled lemon-
        pepper tuna kebabs
        with, 150–51
    herb, grilled tuna and
        peppers sandwich with,
        160–61
    in a new shrimp cocktail,
        3
mesclun, seared salmon and
    raspberry vermouth
    vinaigrette with, 106–7
mint chutney, grilled
    tandoori-style shrimp
    with, 18–19
mushroom(s):
    caps, salmon-stuffed
        Portobello, 84–85
    and swordfish Marsala,
        144–45
mustard dressing, salmon
    cobb salad with creamy,
    102–3

noodle(s):
    and cabbage slaw, sweet-
        and-sour, 200–201
    egg, with tomato, 177
nut-crusted halibut, 127

Old Bay Seasoning:
    in a new shrimp cocktail,
        3
    in Old Bay seasoned
        roasted new potatoes,
        171
    in simply spiced shrimp,
        44
olives:
    in fresh tuna salad,
        166–65

in roasted salmon
puttanesca, 83
one-dish meals:
roasted shrimp, potatoes,
and prosciutto
Portuguese-style, 33
shrimp, jicama, and
avocado salad with
cumin grapefruit
dressing, 4–5
shrimp and sausage
jambalaya, 36–37
shrimp pot pie, 54–55
onion(s):
caramelized, cauliflower
with poppy seeds and,
185
and cucumber salad with
yogurt cumin
vinaigrette, 202–3
in egg noodles with
tomato, 177
fried, crisp salmon on
lentils with, 78–79
Mexican pickled, chili-
rubbed halibut with,
114–15
sweet, curried shrimp
with, 46
swordfish with raisins,
pine nuts and,
132–33
wine sauce, roasted
halibut with, 118–19
orange:
-glazed shrimp with
gingered cucumber
salsa, 20–21
in grilled salmon steaks
on citrus, 66–67
overfishing, xv-xvi

pasta:
shrimp and artichoke
fettuccini Alfredo,
40–41
in shrimp in Greek
tomato herb and feta
sauce, 38–39

shrimp with broccoli
rabe, bacon and, 42–43
toasted vermicelli and
herbs, 176
see also noodle(s)
peanut dip, cilantro shrimp
with, 6–7
peas:
in blasted vegetables, 188
and rye croutons, 190
peppered salmon, 65
peppers, see bell pepper(s);
green chili; jalapeño
pepper(s)
pickled shrimp with wasabi,
12–13
pie:
salmon, with roasted
peppers, leeks, and
horseradish, 86–87
shrimp pot, 54–55
pineapple:
and carrot salsa, curried
swordfish kebabs with,
138–39
fried rice with ham and,
179
scallion-butter sauce,
grilled butterflied
shrimp with, 24–25
pine nuts, swordfish with
onions, raisins and,
132–33
pita:
shrimp stuffed with
spinach, sun-dried
tomatoes, almonds and,
34–35
sticks, 208
plantains, broiled ripe,
194–95
poached, xvii
salmon, in lemon tomato
broth, 96–97
salmon, in sake with
celery and ginger, 94
salmon, simply, 95
salmon with cucumber-
yogurt sauce, 108–9

swordfish, in curried tomato
sauce, 134–35
pomegranate seeds,
swordfish in curried
pumpkin sauce with
sunflower and, 142–43
poppy seeds, cauliflower
with caramelized
onions and, 185
port, seared tuna with figs
and, 156–57
Portobello mushroom caps,
salmon-stuffed, 84–85
potato(es):
-crusted halibut with
chive sour cream sauce,
116–17
Old Bay seasoned roasted
new, 171
shrimp, and prosciutto,
Portuguese-style,
roasted, 33
skinny scalloped, 172–73
tuna roasted on leeks,
sage and, 162–63
prosciutto, shrimp, and
potatoes, Portuguese-
style, roasted, 33
pumpkin sauce, curried,
with sunflower and
pomegranate seeds,
swordfish in, 142–43

quick rice and beans, 178

raisins, swordfish with pine
nuts and, 132–33
rice:
in Asian-style salmon
lettuce rolls, 104–5
Basmati, currant, and
carrot salad, 180–81
and beans, quick, 178
fried, with ham and
pineapple, 179
in shrimp and sausage
jambalaya, 36–37
in stir-fried shrimp and
broccoli, 28–29

roasted, xvii
  halibut with onion wine
    sauce, 118–19
  salmon pie, 86–87
  salmon puttanesca, 83
  shrimp, potatoes, and
    prosciutto Portuguese-
    style, 33
  swordfish Cuban-style,
    136
  tuna on leeks, potatoes,
    and sage, 162–63

sage, tuna roasted on leeks,
  potatoes and, 162–63
sake with ginger and celery,
  salmon poached in, 94
salads:
  Basmati rice, currant, and
    carrot, 180–81
  cucumbers and onion,
    with yogurt cumin
    vinaigrette, 202–3
  fresh tuna, 166–65
  green, with grapes and
    walnuts, 205
  grilled ratatouille, 186–87
  salmon cobb, with creamy
    mustard dressing, 102–3
  seared salmon with
    mesclun and raspberry
    vermouth vinaigrette,
    106–7
  tsatsiki shrimp, 32
salmon, xiii-xiv
  baked, with apricots and
    water chestnuts, 89
  baked, with bell pepper
    salsa, 82
  baked, with deviled-egg
    sauce, 90–91
  blackened, on zesty
    cabbage, 74–75
  cobb salad with creamy
    mustard dressing, 102–3
  crisp, on lentils with fried
    onions, 78–79
  crispy, on tangerine and
    bacon spinach, 62–63

and fennel under wraps,
  92–93
in grape sauce, 98–99
in green chili cream,
  70–71
grilled, steaks on citrus,
  66–67
grilled, with green chili
  coconut sauce, 68–69
grilled molasses, with
  lime, 64
jerk-spiced, steaks, 60–61
lettuce rolls, Asian-style,
  104–5
in mock tamarind sauce,
  100–101
peppered, 65
pie with roasted peppers,
  leeks, and horseradish,
  86–87
poached, with cucumber-
  yogurt sauce, 108–9
poached in lemon tomato
  broth, 96–97
poached in sake with
  ginger and celery, 94
roasted, puttanesca, 83
roasted in garlic butter, 88
sautéed, smothered in
  summer (tomatoes and
  basil), 80–81
sautéed, with asparagus
  and chickpea
  vinaigrette, 72–73
seared, with mesclun and
  raspberry vermouth
  vinaigrette, 106–7
sesame-crusted, teriyaki,
  58–59
simply poached, 95
slow-fried herbed, in
  extra-virgin olive oil,
  76–77
-stuffed Portobello
  mushroom caps, 84–85
and yellow pepper
  chowder, 110–11
salsa:
  bell pepper, with baked
    salmon, 82

black bean, 206
fresh tomato, 207
gingered cucumber, with
  orange-glazed shrimp,
  20–21
pineapple and carrot, with
  curried swordfish
  kebabs, 138–39
sandwich, grilled tuna and
  peppers, with herb
  mayonnaise, 160–61
sauces:
  for Big-Easy shrimp,
    26–27
  black bean, sautéed
    shrimp with, 14–15
  carrot and basil, grilled
    tuna marinated in,
    158–59
  chive sour cream, potato-
    crusted halibut with,
    116–17
  cucumber-yogurt,
    poached salmon with,
    108–9
  curried pumpkin,
    swordfish in, with
    sunflower and
    pomegranate seeds,
    142–43
  curried tomato, swordfish
    poached in, 134–35
  deviled-egg, salmon baked
    with, 90–91
  garlic caramel, tuna in,
    164–65
  grape, salmon in, 98–99
  Greek tomato herb and
    feta, shrimp in, 38–39
  green chili coconut,
    grilled salmon with,
    68–69
  lemon, halibut in, 126
  mock tamarind, salmon
    in, 100–101
  onion wine, roasted
    halibut with, 118–19
  pineapple scallion-butter,
    grilled butterflied
    shrimp with, 24–25

roasted jalapeño tartar,
halibut steak baked
with, 122–23
for roasted salmon
puttanesca, 83
for simply boiled shrimp,
3
tahini parsley, grilled tuna
with, 152–53
see also chutney; salsa
sausage(s):
in collard greens with a
northern accent, 204
and shrimp jambalaya,
36–37
sautéed, xvii
fennel and apples, 189
salmon smothered in
summer (tomatoes and
basil), 80–81
salmon with asparagus
and chickpea
vinaigrette, 72–73
shrimp with black bean
sauce, 14–15
scallion-butter pineapple
sauce with grilled
butterflied shrimp,
24–25
seafood:
buying of, x-xi
cooking of, xvi-xvii
see also specific fish
seared:
salmon with mesclun and
raspberry vermouth
vinaigrette, 106–7
tuna with port and figs,
156–57
sesame-crusted salmon
teriyaki, 58–59
shark:
grilled Korean-style,
154–55
grilled lemon-pepper,
kebabs with chive
mayonnaise, 150–51
shrimp, xi-xiii, xviii-xix, 2–55
and artichoke fettuccini
Alfredo, 40–41

baked, pesto, 30–31
Big-Easy, 26–27
and broccoli, stir-fried,
28–29
with broccoli rabe, bacon,
and pasta, 42–43
Buffalo, 8–9
Caesar, tomato, and
artichoke heart kebabs,
22–23
cilantro, with peanut dip,
6–7
cocktail, a new, 3
cornmeal fried, 47
crisp coconut graham,
52–53
crisp sesame, 50–51
curried, with sweet
onions, 46
deviled, 48–49
in Greek tomato herb and
feta sauce, 38–39
grilled, wrapped in hot
cappicola and basil,
16–17
grilled butterflied, with
pineapple scallion-
butter sauce, 24–25
grilled margarita, fajitas,
10–11
grilled tandoori-style, with
mint chutney, 18–19
jerk-spiced, 60–61
jicama, and avocado salad
with cumin grapefruit
dressing, 4–5
orange-glazed, with
gingered cucumber
salsa, 20–21
pickled, with wasabi,
12–13
potatoes, and prosciutto
Portuguese-style,
roasted, 33
pot pie, 54–55
and sausage jambalaya,
36–37
sautéed, with black bean
sauce, 14–15
simply boiled, 2

simply spiced, 44–45
stuffed with pita, spinach,
sun-dried tomatoes and
almonds, 34–35
tsatsiki salad, 32
side dishes, 168–208
blasted sweet potatoes
with salt, malt vinegar,
and parsley, 170
blasted vegetables, 188
braised escarole with
tomatoes and garlic, 184
broiled ripe plantains,
194–95
cauliflower with
caramelized onions and
poppy seeds, 185
charred soy and sesame
string beans, 183
collard greens with a
northern accent, 204
couscous with dried
cranberries and
buttered almonds, 175
cucumber and onion
salad with yogurt cumin
vinaigrette, 202–3
fried corn and peppers
with butter and basil,
191
gingered spaghetti
squash, 196–97
green salad with grapes
and walnuts, 205
grilled ratatouille salad,
186–87
herbed Parmesan grits,
174
mashed white beans and
garlic, 182
Old Bay seasoned roasted
new potatoes, 171
peas and rye croutons, 190
sautéed fennel and
apples, 189
skinny scalloped potatoes,
172–73
watercress with balsamic
vinegar and butter, 193
zesty asparagus, 192

side dishes: (*cont.*)
  zucchini casserole,
    198–99
  see also noodle(s); pasta;
    rice
simply boiled shrimp, in
  tsatsiki shrimp salad, 32
simply poached salmon, 95
simply spiced shrimp, 44–45
skinny scalloped potatoes,
  172–73
slow-fried herbed salmon in
  extra-virgin olive oil,
  76–77
spaghetti squash, gingered,
  196–97
spinach:
  with balsamic vinegar and
    butter, 193
  crispy salmon on
    tangerine and bacon,
    62–63
  with grapes and walnuts,
    205
  shrimp stuffed with pita,
    sun-dried tomatoes,
    almonds and, 34–35
  shrimp with bacon, pasta
    and, 42–43
steaming seafood, xvii
stewing, xvii
  halibut stewed with
    tomatoes and white
    beans, 124–25
stir-fried shrimp and
  broccoli, 28–29
sunflower seeds, swordfish
  in curried pumpkin
  sauce with pomegranate
  and, 142–43
sweet, hot, and sour chutney
  sauce, 53
sweet-and-sour noodle and
  cabbage slaw, 200–201
sweet potatoes, blasted, with
  salt, malt vinegar, and
  parsley, 170
Swiss chard, shrimp with
  bacon, pasta and, 42–43
swordfish, xiv, xv–xvi

chili-rubbed, with
  Mexican pickled onions,
  114–15
curried, kebabs with
  pineapple and carrot
  salsa, 138–39
in curried pumpkin sauce
  with sunflower and
  pomegranate seeds,
  142–43
grilled, *see* swordfish,
  grilled
marinade, 58–59
marmalade-marinated,
  140–41
and mushroom Marsala,
  144–45
with onions, raisins, and
  pine nuts, 132–33
poached in curried
  tomato sauce, 134–35
roasted, Cuban-style,
  136
roasted on leeks, potatoes,
  and sage, 162–63
schnitzel, 146
sesame-crusted, teriyaki,
  58–59
stewed with tomatoes and
  white beans, 124–25
swordfish, grilled:
  Dijon, 147
  in flank steak marinade,
    137
  Korean-style, 154–55
  lemon-pepper, kebabs
    with chive mayonnaise,
    150–51
  marinated in basil and
    carrot sauce, 158–59
  molasses, with lime, 64
  sangria, 148–49
  with tahini parsley sauce,
    152–53

tahini parsley sauce, grilled
  tuna with, 152–53
tamarind sauce, mock,
  salmon in, 100–101

tangerine, crispy salmon on
  bacon spinach and,
  62–63
toasted vermicelli and
  herbs, 176
tomato(es):
  braised escarole with
    garlic and, 184
  Caesar shrimp, and
    artichoke heart kebabs,
    22–23
  egg noodles with, 177
  in grilled ratatouille,
    186–87
  halibut stewed with white
    beans and, 124–25
  herb and feta sauce,
    shrimp in Greek, 38–39
  lemon broth, salmon
    poached in, 96–97
  in roasted salmon
    puttanesca, 83
  salsa, fresh, 207
  sauce, curried, swordfish
    poached in, 134–35
  in sautéed salmon
    smothered in summer
    (tomatoes and basil),
    80–81
  in shrimp with broccoli
    rabe, bacon and pasta,
    42–43
  sun-dried, shrimp stuffed
    with pita, spinach,
    almonds and, 34–35
tsatsiki shrimp salad, 32
tuna, xiv-xv
  chili-rubbed, with
    Mexican pickled onions,
    114–15
  in garlic caramel sauce,
    164–65
  grilled, *see* tuna, grilled
  marinade, 58–59
  marmalade-marinated,
    140–41
  with onions, raisins, and
    pine nuts, 132–33
  poached in curried
    tomato sauce, 134–35

roasted, Cuban-style,
136
roasted on leeks, potatoes,
and sage, 162–63
salad, fresh, 166–65
seared, with port and figs,
156–57
sesame-crusted, teriyaki,
58–59
stewed with tomatoes
and white beans,
124–25
tuna, grilled:
Dijon, 147
in flank steak marinade,
137
Korean-style, 154–55
lemon-pepper, kebabs
with chive mayonnaise,
150–51
marinated in carrot and
basil sauce, 158–59

and peppers sandwich
with herb mayonnaise,
160–61
sangria, 148–49
with tahini parsley sauce,
152–53

vinaigrettes:
asparagus and chickpea,
sautéed salmon with,
72–73
raspberry vermouth,
seared salmon with
mesclun and, 106–7
yogurt cumin, cucumber
and onion salad with,
202–3

walnuts, green salad with
grapes and, 205
wasabi with pickled shrimp,
12–13

water chestnuts, salmon
baked with apricots
and, 89
watercress with balsamic
vinegar and butter,
193
white beans, halibut stewed
with tomatoes and,
124–25

yellow pepper and
salmon chowder,
110–11
yogurt-cucumber sauce,
poached salmon with,
108–9

zesty asparagus, 192
zucchini:
casserole, 198–99
in grilled ratatouille,
186–87